Simply Delicious
Versatile Vegetables

Darina Allen

Gill & Macmillan
Radio Telefís Éireann

Published by
Gill & Macmillan Ltd
Goldenbridge
Dublin 8
and
Radio Telefís Éireann
Donnybrook
Dublin 4

© *Darina Allen 1994*
0 7171 2152 6

Photographs by Des Gaffney/RTE
Food styling by Rory O'Connell
Designed by Identikit Design Consultants, Dublin
Colour origination by Kulor Centre, Dublin
Printed by ColourBooks Ltd, Dublin

A catalogue record for this book is available from the British Library.

5 7 9 10 8 6 4

For my garden angels – Eileen, Elizabeth and Haulie

Contents

Asparagus

Aubergines

Beans, Broad

Beans, French and Runner

Beetroot

Broccoli or Calabrese

Brussels Sprouts

Cabbage

Carrots

Cauliflower

Celery

Courgettes and Marrows

Cucumber

Globe Artichokes

Jerusalem Artichokes

Leeks

Lettuce and Salad Leaves

Mixed Vegetable Dishes

Mushrooms

Onions and Garlic

Parsnips

Peas

Peppers and Chillies

Potatoes

Spinach and Swiss Chard

Sweetcorn

Tomatoes

Turnips

* Recipes demonstrated on RTE's *Simply Delicious Versatile Vegetables* television series
ᵛ Recipes suitable for non-vegan vegetarians
ᵛᵛ Recipes suitable for vegans

Foreword

The first thing I should stress is that *Simply Delicious Versatile Vegetables* isn't just for vegetarians, though of course I hope that vegetarians will enjoy it. In fact it is for everybody who is intrigued by the new and exciting possibilities vegetables offer. There are more varieties than ever in our shops, with exotic new arrivals almost every week – and vegetables are so extraordinarily versatile that there is no limit to the number of interesting dishes they inspire.

I have always felt that vegetables have been treated rather unfairly as the poor relation to meat or fish. Traditionally, that lack of respect has carried through to the cooking. There has been a tendency to boil them to a mush, obliterating every last vestige of natural flavour. Not much wonder people have found it difficult to see their potential!

But now the time has come to take a completely new look at vegetables and let them star in their own right. Suddenly, leading chefs are experimenting with all sorts of wonderful new vegetable ideas, trying out daring new combinations and a whole range of cooking methods – baking, roasting, chargrilling or wrapping them in pastry instead of just boiling them to bits.

As the new emphasis on vegetable cookery gathers momentum, there is a reawakening of interest in traditional root vegetables which, not so long ago, wouldn't have been considered fit for any restaurant menu. I am delighted that so many trendy restaurants in London have rediscovered carrots, swede turnips and parsnips, and found irresistible ways of proving how delicious they can be.

Vegetables are usually excellent value for money. They are also extremely healthy. I know parents often worry that vegetarian children may be missing out on essential nutrients, especially if they are in their teens (and there is no doubt that the number of teenage vegetarians in Ireland has increased dramatically in the past few years). With a little forethought about protein and calcium sources, however, it is quite easy to provide interesting and nutritious meals, not just for vegetarians but also for vegans. Remember that entire nations – a large proportion of those who live on the Indian sub-continent, for instance – survive perfectly well on a vegetarian diet! Don't seize up at the very thought of having to cook for a vegetarian, because, as I think this book demonstrates, there really are lots and lots of wonderful recipes you can try.

In my ideal world, everybody would have the opportunity to grow their own vegetables, not just in order to save money but for the sheer pleasure of it. Once you sow a packet of seeds and watch your first plants grow, I guarantee you will be hooked! No vegetables taste as good as the ones that have come straight from your own garden, and the great bonus is that they are there for you to enjoy at all the different stages of their development.

Even a small plot, 10ft by 10ft, can produce a surprising amount, so I would advise new gardeners not to be overambitious but to start in a small way. If space is limited, you might join forces with a few neighbours, decide to plant different things and share the results. You can also try planting herbs and tiny viola flowers for salads in a window box, or have tumbler tomatoes dangling enticingly from a hanging basket. If you do go to the trouble of growing your own vegetables, it is worth trying to garden as organically as possible so that you achieve the best results for your hard work.

For non-gardeners, the next best thing is to buy organically grown produce where possible, and of course to be aware of the different varieties available, as their flavour can differ enormously. Buy locally grown vegetables if you can. I am a firm believer in the principle that if we all put money back into our own area it will bear fruit in the future – and apart from that, vegetables from the locality are likely to be fresh, cheap and in season.

At the very least, for goodness sake let's all buy Irish every time we can, rather than spend money on imported vegetables out of season. There is precious little food value or flavour left in anything that has been in transit for two or three weeks. To make matters worse, these colourless imports are likely to cost two or three times more than vegetables that are here under our noses. By now buying Irish really should be second nature to us all.

I hope *Simply Delicious Versatile Vegetables* will help you, not just to discover how splendid well-cooked vegetables can be as an accompaniment, but to go on and create inspiring meals using all sorts of vegetables in different combinations. The mental block that makes us see vegetables in a supporting role is deeply ingrained – but once you get over that you will have opened the kitchen door to a whole new culinary world. I can assure you that there are far more delicious vegetable dishes than I was able to include here. As usual, shortage of space curbed my enthusiasm! Still, I hope *Simply Delicious Versatile Vegetables* will be useful as a springboard to help you dream up wonderful creations of your own.

Here's to the green Nineties, and a whole, exciting new vegetable era!

Darina Allen
Shanagarry
Co. Cork
November 1993

Acknowledgments

The research for *Simply Delicious Versatile Vegetables* yielded unexpected pleasures. Travelling all over Ireland with my indomitable RTE crew, I unearthed vegetable growers whose skill and dedication impressed me as much as the superb quality of their produce.

At Hilton Park in Co. Monaghan, one of Ireland's loveliest country house hotels, Lucy Madden turns the vegetables and herbs she grows organically into exquisite food that makes you want to visit Hilton over and over again. At Eden Herbs in Co. Leitrim, Rod Alston and his helpers have created a little oasis in challenging terrain. Possibly the largest selection of herbs in Ireland and abundant crops of vegetables are cultivated with great humour and sold, both to local restaurants and to the Leitrim Growers Co-op shop in Manorhamilton which has as fine a selection of organic vegetables and fruit on offer as you'll find anywhere.

Another minor miracle has been achieved in the tiny village of Cornamona at the top of Lough Corrib. Here Norita Clesham and Anne Coyne, helped by Dolores Keegan, a founder of Eden Herbs, run An t-Inneall Glas, an EC-funded project to teach rural women how to grow organically in soil even more challenging than in Leitrim. The raised beds, dug into heavy, waterlogged soil, looked as though they should have been growing rice rather than the fantastic selection of vegetables and fruit that appeared to be flourishing. The enthusiasm of everyone involved was infectious.

In Kilkilleen in West Cork there was Bob Allen, whose beautiful organically grown vegetables can be ordered direct from the farm. Many organic growers are encouraging people to buy vegetables in this way, among them the dynamic West Wicklow Growers. In the Baltinglass area a cluster of organic farmers – Denis Healy, Penny and Udo Lange, Hilda Crampton, Dominic Quinn – produce wonderful vegetables with impressive efficiency and deliver them daily to the Dublin market and to Organic Foods in Lucan.

As ever, I am deeply grateful to my own extensive team of helpers, without whose invaluable assistance and forbearance no book or television series would ever emerge as anything resembling an organic whole!

I would particularly like to thank: Ivan and Myrtle Allen; Tim Allen; Roy Bedell; Tony Cournane; Claire Cullinane; Kevin Cummins; Rosalie Dunne; Colette Farmer; Gary Finnegan; Des Gaffney; Claire Kelly; Joe Kerins; Adrienne Morrissey; Breda Murphy; Rory O'Connell; Denis O'Farrell; Brian O'Mahony; Rachel O'Neill; Miriam O'Shea; John Rogers.

Glossary

Al dente: To cook pasta or vegetables until firm to the bite.

Bake blind: Line a pastry case with kitchen paper, and fill to the top with baking beans. Prebake for 15-20 minutes in a moderate oven.

Blanch: This cooking term can be confusing because it is used in many different senses. Usually it means to immerse food in water and to bring to the boil, parcook, extract salt or to loosen skins as in the case of almonds.

Bouquet garni: A small bunch of fresh herbs used to flavour stews, casseroles, stocks or soups, usually consisting of parsley stalks, a sprig of thyme, perhaps a bay leaf and an outside stalk of celery. Remove before serving.

Clarified butter: Melt butter on a very low heat, allow to settle then skim off the frothy top. The clear liquid is clarified butter which can be brought to a higher temperature than ordinary butter.

Degorge: To sprinkle salt on vegetables, e.g. cucumber or aubergine, to draw out the excess liquid or bitter juices.

Degrease: To remove surplus fat from a liquid or a pan, either by pouring off or by skimming the surface with a spoon.

Egg wash: A raw egg beaten with a pinch of salt, it is brushed on raw tarts, pies and biscuits to give them a shiny, golden glaze when cooked.

Paper lid: When we are sweating vegetables for the base of a soup or stew, we quite often cover them with a butter wrapper or a lid made from greaseproof paper which fits the saucepan exactly. This keeps in the steam and helps to sweat the vegetables.

Roux: Equal quantities of butter and flour cooked together for 2 minutes over a gentle heat. This mixture may be whisked into boiling liquid to thicken, e.g. gravies, sauces, milk.

Scald: (a) To heat milk or cream to just below boiling point, or (b) to plunge fruit or vegetables in boiling water to remove the skins.

Measurements

All imperial spoon measurements in this book are rounded measurements unless the recipe states otherwise. All American spoon measurements are level.

Temperature Conversion

Approximate fahrenheit/centigrade equivalents are given in the recipes, but for fan or convection ovens it is wise to check the manufacturer's instructions regarding temperature conversion.

Gardening Books

For really keen gardeners who like to experiment with unusual vegetables or like to source oldfashioned varieties there is one book that I find invaluable, the *Veg Finder* published by the Henry Doubleday Research Association and distributed by Moorland Publishing Co. Ltd, Moor Farm Road, Airfield, Airfield Estate, Ashbourne, Derbyshire DE6 1HD – about £5.99 in specialist bookshops.

For people who are committed to growing organically, the book I would recommend is *The Organic Gardener* by Bob Flowerdew.

Seed Suppliers

- Suttons Seeds, exclusive agents in Ireland, Goldcrop Ltd, John F. Kennedy Park, Killeen Road, Dublin 12. Phone: 01 504388, Fax: 01 505650.
- Thompson & Morgan, distributed in Ireland by Mr Middleton, Garden Shop, Royal Hibernian Way, South Anne Street, Dublin 2. Phone: 01 6797602.
- Europrise Co. Ltd, Vegetable Seed Specialist, Blakes Cross, Lusk, Co. Dublin. Phone: 01 438711, Fax: 438702.
- Suffolk Herbs, Monks Farm, Pantlings Lane, Kelvedon, Essex CO5 9PG, England. Phone: 0044 376 572456, Fax: 0044 376 571189.
- Unwins Seeds Ltd, Mail Order Department, Histon, Cambridge CB4 4ZZ. Phone: 0044 920 870811.
- Mrs M. Mac Lean, Dornock Farm, Crieff, Perthshire PH7 3QN, Scotland. Phone: 0044 764 2472. Wonderful range of potatoes.
- Chiltern Seeds, Bortree Stile, Ulverston, Cumbria LA12 7PB, England. Phone: 0044 229 581137, Fax 0044 229 54549.
- Future Foods, 3 Tai Madog, Stablau, Llanrug, Gwynedd LL5 3PH, Wales. Phone: 0044 286 870606.
- The Henry Doubleday Research Association, Ryton Organic Gardens, Ryton-on-Dunsmore, Coventry CV8 3LG, England. Suppliers of oldfashioned and rare seeds, they also have a seed bank. Phone: 0044 203 303517, Fax: 0044 203 639229.

Asparagus

The aristocrat of vegetables is worth growing but tries your patience more than most. You must resist the temptation to harvest it for two or three years in order to build up strong, healthy crowns – but at least you'll have the benefit of beautiful, feathery foliage. After that, provided you have planted it in good, rich soil, you will be able to pick lots of fat green spears from the beginning of May onwards. The good news for non-gardeners is that asparagus is now much more widely available than previously – and over a much longer season.

^v Asparagus Bundles with Hollandaise, Mousseline or Maltaise Sauce

This is a rather fancy way to serve asparagus. You could dispense with the ties and just serve the asparagus with the sauce if you like.

1½–2 lbs (675–900 g) fresh Irish asparagus
1 leek *or* some chives
Hollandaise Sauce (see below) *or* Mousseline Sauce (see below) *or* Maltaise Sauce (see below)

Garnish
Chervil

Serves 4

Wash the leek (if using) and cut in half lengthwise. Blanch and refresh under cold water. Drain on kitchen paper. Peel and trim the root end of the asparagus. Cut into uniform lengths and save the trimmings for soup.

Make the sauce and keep warm.

Just before serving, cook the asparagus in boiling salted water. If you have a special asparagus pot, that's wonderful, but you can manage

1

very well without it. Depending on the thickness of the spears it may take from 8 to 12 minutes to cook. Test by putting the tip of a sharp knife through the thicker end. Remove from the water and drain.

Tie the asparagus into bundles of 3 or 5 with the strips of leek or chives. Put a generous tablespoonful of Hollandaise, Mousseline or Maltaise Sauce on each warm plate and place the asparagus bundle on top. Garnish with chervil and serve immediately.

^V HOLLANDAISE SAUCE

2 egg yolks, preferably free-range
4 ozs (110 g/1 stick) butter
1 dessertsp. (2 American teasp.)
cold water
1 teasp. approx. lemon juice

Serves 4-6, depending on what it is to accompany. Goes well with poached fish, eggs and vegetables.

Put the egg yolks into a heavy stainless steel saucepan on a low heat, or in a bowl over hot water. Add the water and whisk thoroughly. Add the butter bit by bit, whisking all the time. As soon as one piece melts, add the next piece. The mixture will gradually thicken, but if it shows signs of becoming too thick or slightly 'scrambling', remove from the heat immediately and add a little cold water if necessary. Do not leave the pan or stop whisking until the sauce is made. Finally add the lemon juice to taste.

If the sauce is slow to thicken it may be because you are excessively cautious and the heat is too low. Increase the heat slightly and continue to whisk until the sauce thickens to coating consistency. However, it is important to remember that if you are making Hollandaise Sauce in a saucepan directly over the heat, it should be possible to put your hand on the side of the saucepan at any stage. If the saucepan feels too hot for your hand, it is also too hot for the sauce.

Another good tip if you are making Hollandaise Sauce for the first time is to keep a bowl of cold water close by, so that you can plunge the bottom of the saucepan into the bowl if it becomes too hot.

Keep the sauce warm until service, either in a bowl over hot but not boiling water, or in a thermos flask. Hollandaise Sauce should not be reheated. Left-over sauce may be used as an enrichment for cream sauces, or mashed potatoes, or to perk up a fish pie etc.

V MOUSSELINE SAUCE

Whisk 2½ fl ozs (63 ml/generous ¼ cup) cream until fairly stiff and fold carefully into the Hollandaise Sauce just before serving. Correct the seasoning.

V MALTAISE SAUCE

Blood oranges are best for this sauce but they may be difficult to find at some times of the year.

Add the juice and most of the rind of 1 small orange, preferably a blood orange, to the Hollandaise Sauce just before serving. Make sure to scrub the rind of the orange well before grating.

VV Roast Asparagus with Sea Salt

*T*his rather bizarre way of cooking asparagus comes to us from California. Roast asparagus may sound unlikely, but its flavour is wonderfully intense and particularly good served as part of a plate which includes Chargrilled Red and Yellow Peppers (see page 103), Aubergine slices, chargrilled onions and Courgettes with Marjoram (see page 49).

1 bunch of fresh Irish asparagus
**1 tablesp. approx. extra virgin
   olive oil**
sea salt (Maldon if possible)

Serves 4

Trim the asparagus and peel the root ends with a swivel top peeler. Drizzle the spears with a little olive oil. Toss gently to coat, season with sea salt, put on to a roasting tin and roast in a hot oven, 230°C/450°F/regulo 8, for 8-10 minutes.

Serve with crusty bread.

V Roast Asparagus with Sea Salt and Parmesan

Sprinkle a little freshly grated Parmesan cheese, preferably Parmigiano Reggiano, and sea salt over the roast asparagus (previous recipe) and eat immediately. Completely exquisite!

^V Tagliatelle with Cream and Asparagus

Wickedly rich but utterly delicious once a year!

8 ozs (225 g) fresh Irish asparagus
8 ozs (225 g) tagliatelle,
    preferably fresh and
    homemade
4 pints (2.3 L/10 cups) water
2 large tablespoons salt
1 oz (30 g/¼ stick) butter
6 ozs (170 g/¾ cup) best quality
    cream
2 ozs (55 g/½ cup) freshly grated
    Parmesan cheese, preferably
    Parmigiano Reggiano
freshly ground pepper, nutmeg
    and sea salt

Serves 4 as a main course

Snap off the root end of the asparagus where it breaks naturally; cook the asparagus in boiling salted water until *al dente*, drain and save.

Bring the water to a good rolling boil, add the salt and drop in the tagliatelle; cover the pot for just a few seconds until the water comes back to the boil. Cook the tagliatelle until barely *al dente* (remember it will cook a little more in the pan). Homemade tagliatelle will take only 1-2 minutes whereas bought pasta will take considerably longer – 10-12 minutes depending on the brand.

Cut the asparagus into thin slices at an angle (no thicker than ¼ inch/ 5 mm). Melt the butter in a wide saucepan, add half the cream and simmer for a couple of minutes just until the cream thickens slightly; then add the asparagus, the hot drained tagliatelle, the rest of the cream and the cheese. Season with freshly ground pepper, nutmeg and sea salt. Toss briefly – just enough to coat the pasta, taste and add a little more seasoning if necessary. Serve immediately.

^V Asparagus and Spring Onion Tart

My children and their friends reckon that Tim makes the best quiches in the whole world. They are not biased – he does. Try this one!

Shortcrust Pastry
4 ozs (110 g/scant 1 cup) white
    flour
2 ozs (55 g/½ stick) butter
1 egg, preferably free-range

Filling
5 ozs (140 g) asparagus, trimmed
    and with ends peeled
½ oz (15 g/1 tablesp.) butter
1 tablesp. (1 American tablesp. +
    1 teasp.) olive oil
9 ozs (255 g/scant 2 cups) onion,
    finely chopped (we use about
    half spring onion complete
    with green tops and half
    ordinary onion)

**4 ozs (110 g/1 cup) Irish Cheddar
    cheese, grated**
3 eggs, preferably free–range
4 fl ozs (120 ml/½ cup) cream
salt and freshly ground pepper

**1 × 7 inch (18 cm) quiche tin *or*
    1 × 7 inch (18 cm) flan ring**

Serves 6

Make the shortcrust pastry in the
usual way (see page 122). Line the
flan ring or quiche tin with the pastry
and bake blind for 20 minutes
approx. in a moderate oven,
180°C/350°F/ regulo 4. Remove the
beans, egg wash the base and return
to the oven for 1-2 minutes. This
seals the pastry and helps to avoid a
'soggy bottom'.

Melt the butter, add the olive oil
and onions; sweat the onions with a
good pinch of salt until soft but not
coloured.

Cook the asparagus in boiling
salted water until *al dente*, then drain.
When it is cool enough to handle,
cut into ½ inch (1 cm) pieces.

Whisk the eggs in a bowl, add the
cream, almost all the cheese, onion
and the cooked asparagus. Season
with salt and freshly ground pepper.
Pour into the pastry case, sprinkle the
remainder of the cheese on top and
bake in a moderate oven, 180°C/
350°F/regulo 4, for 40-45 minutes.

Aubergines

^v Aubergines with Various Toppings
^{v*} Aubergines with Pesto
^v Justin's Aubergine and Mozzarella Sandwich
*^{vv} The Lake Palace Hotel's Aubergines
cooked in Pickling Style*

If you are hooked on growing things and have a greenhouse, aubergines are terrifically rewarding because, quite apart from the vegetable itself, the plant is very attractive with the prettiest purple flowers. The other great advantage of growing aubergines is that you can try the many varieties which still unfortunately haven't made their way into Irish shops – from the large Black Beauty right down to the little Pea Aubergine so beloved of Thais and Indonesians. It has to be admitted that the slightly smoky taste of aubergines is an acquired taste – but half of the Middle East and most of India can't be wrong! When you are converted you will find that there are literally hundreds of recipes to try.

^v Aubergines with Various Toppings

For most recipes, start by cutting the aubergines into ½ inch (1 cm) thick slices, either lengthwise or in rounds. Then sprinkle them lightly with salt, stand them upright in a colander and allow to drain for 30 minutes approx.

To cook: Wash and dry the aubergine slices well. Heat about ¾ inch (2 cm) olive oil in a frying pan until it is hot but not smoking. Fry a few slices at a time until golden on both sides. Drain on a wire rack over a baking sheet and then serve in one of the following ways.

^v AUBERGINES WITH TOMATO FONDUE AND/OR PESTO

Put a spoonful of hot or cold Tomato Fondue (see page 15) on each piece of aubergine and serve immediately; or if you prefer, top each one with a small blob of Pesto (see opposite).

^v AUBERGINES WITH TOMATO AND MOZZARELLA

Put a spoonful of Tomato Fondue on each piece of fried aubergine, top it with a slice of Mozzarella cheese (Mozzarella di Bufala if possible) and sprinkle with a little freshly grated Parmesan cheese. Bake in a hot oven for 5 minutes or flash under a grill until the cheese becomes bubbly and golden.

^v AUBERGINES WITH TOMATO, MOZZARELLA AND PESTO

Put a little Pesto (see below) on top of the Tomato Fondue and proceed as above.

^{v*} Aubergines with Pesto

2 aubergines
salt
extra virgin olive oil
Pesto

Serves 4

Split the aubergines in half lengthwise. Score the flesh lightly with a sharp knife, sprinkle with salt and allow to degorge, skin side up on a wire rack, for 20 minutes approx. Rinse under the cold tap and dry with kitchen paper.

Preheat the oven to 220°C/425°F/regulo 7. Put the aubergine halves on to a baking sheet, drizzle with olive oil and bake for 20 minutes approx. Then remove from the oven, spread a spoonful of Pesto on top, flash under the grill and serve immediately.

PESTO
4 ozs (110 g) fresh basil leaves
4 fl ozs (120 ml/½ cup) olive oil
1 oz (30 g) fresh pine kernels
2 large cloves of garlic, crushed
2 ozs (55 g/½ cup) freshly and finely grated Parmesan cheese, preferably Parmigiano Reggiano
salt

In a food processor, whizz the basil with the olive oil, pine kernels and garlic, or pound them in a pestle and mortar. Remove to a bowl and fold in the Parmesan cheese. Taste and season. Pesto keeps for weeks, covered with a layer of olive oil, in a jar in the fridge. It also freezes well but for best results don't add the grated Parmesan until it has defrosted. Freeze in small jars for convenience.

7

^v Justin's Aubergine and Mozzarella Sandwich

This was inspired by a delicious 'sandwich' I ate at Zoe, one of Antony Worrall-Thompson's innovative restaurants in London.

1 medium sized aubergine
salt and freshly ground pepper
1 ball of buffalo Mozzarella
2 tablesp. (2 American tablesp. +
  2 teasp.) Pesto (see previous
  recipe)
1 red and 1 yellow pepper,
  roasted, peeled and cut into
  julienne strips (see page 104)
8 fresh basil leaves
extra virgin olive oil
balsamic vinegar

Garnish
chervil and chives
black olives and sundried
  tomatoes (optional)

Serves 4 approx.

Cut the aubergine into ½ inch (1 cm) slices, sprinkle with salt and allow to degorge while you prepare the other ingredients.

Slice the Mozzarella cheese into thin rounds and spread Pesto over the slices. Heat 1 inch (2.5 cm) of olive oil in a frying pan and fry the aubergines on each side until golden brown.

To assemble, heat the roast peppers and aubergine slices if necessary in a hot oven for 3 minutes approx. Place a round of aubergine on a warm plate, season with salt and freshly ground pepper, put a piece of Mozzarella on top, next another piece of aubergine, then some roasted red and yellow pepper, season again, add a leaf or two of basil and then finish with another piece of aubergine. Garnish the top with a little twirl of roasted red and yellow peppers and stick 2 short chives cheekily out of the top.

Be generous with some olive oil and sprinkle it all over the plate, then sprinkle on a little balsamic vinegar. Garnish with a few sprigs of chervil, black olives and little pieces of sundried tomatoes if available. Repeat with the other warm plates.

Serve immediately with lots of crusty Italian bread.

We do many variations on this theme using olive paste, Tomato Fondue (see page 15), sundried tomatoes and rocket, but make sure everything is well seasoned and still warm.

^{vv} The Lake Palace Hotel's Aubergines cooked in Pickling Style

This recipe from Madhur Jaffrey's Indian Cookery is not unlike a spicy ratatouille. It is an exquisite dish. It may be served warm with a leg of lamb or

*a lamb stew but also tastes excellent cold,
served on individual lettuce leaves as a
first course. Sometimes I serve it for lunch
with cold chicken, lamb or ham. It keeps
for ages.*

**1¾ lbs (800 g) aubergines (large *or*
    small variety)**
**1-inch (2.5 cm) cube of fresh
    ginger, peeled and coarsely
    chopped**
6 large cloves of garlic
2 fl ozs (60 ml/¼ cup) water
**12 fl ozs (350 ml/1½ cups)
    approx. vegetable oil (we use
    arachide)**
1 teasp. whole fennel seeds
**½ teasp. kalonji *or* whole cumin
    seeds**
**¾ lb (350 g) tomatoes, peeled and
    finely chopped *or* 1 × 14 oz
    (400 g) tin tomatoes + 1 teasp.
    sugar**
**1 tablesp. (1 American tablesp. +
    1 teasp.) ground coriander
    seeds**
¼ teasp. ground turmeric
**⅓ teasp. cayenne pepper (more if
    you like)**
1¼ teasp. approx. salt

Serves 6

Put the ginger and garlic into the
container of an electric blender or
food processor. Add the water and
blend until fairly smooth.

Cut the aubergines into slices or
wedges ¾ inch (2 cm) thick and
1½–2 inches (4–5 cm) long approx.
Set a sieve over a bowl.

Heat 4 fl ozs (120 ml/½ cup) of
the oil in a deep, 10–12 inch
(25–30 cm) frying pan or saucepan
over a medium-high flame. When
hot, put in as many aubergine slices as
the pan will hold in a single layer. Let
them turn a reddish brown colour on
both sides. Remove the slices to the
sieve. Repeat with the remainder of
the aubergines, adding more oil if
necessary.

While they are draining, put
3 tablespoons approx. of the oil in the
frying pan and heat it over a medium
flame. When hot, put in the fennel
seeds and kalonji or whole cumin. As
soon as the fennel seeds turn a few
shades darker (just a few seconds), put
in the chopped tomatoes, the ginger-
garlic mixture, coriander, turmeric,
cayenne, sugar and salt. Stir and cook
for 5–6 minutes, breaking up the
tomato pieces with the back of a
slotted spoon. Turn up the heat
slightly and continue to stir and cook
until the spice mixture gets thick and
paste-like.

Now put in the fried aubergine
slices and mix gently. Stir very lightly
over a medium-low heat for
5 minutes approx. Cover the pan,
turn the heat to very low and cook
another 5–10 minutes if necessary.

Oil will have collected at the
bottom of the frying pan. Use a
slotted spoon to lift the aubergines
out of this oil when you serve.

Beans, Broad

^vBroad Beans with Summer Savory
[*]Broad Beans with Bacon
Pasta with Broad Beans, Pancetta and Olive Oil

For some reason, broad beans seem to have an image problem. Children often don't like them and, amazingly to me, many adults find them dull. They are one of my absolute favourites, and they hold a special place in many gardeners' hearts because if you plant them in October they will be the first vegetable ready for harvesting, after what seems like a barren eternity.

This year we got even better value out of ours because I discovered that you can eat the tender shoots which have to be pinched out anyway to discourage blackfly. We even made a delicious soup with broad bean tops, from Sophie Grigson's inspiring book *Eat Your Greens*. Both the shoots and the pretty pink, grey and white flowers are delightful in salads.

^v Broad Beans with Summer Savory

Summer savory is a herb which has an extraordinary affinity with beans – it seems to make them taste more 'beany'! If you don't have it, simply leave it out.

1 lb (450 g) shelled broad beans
¼ pint (150 ml/generous ½ cup)
   water
1 teasp. salt
sprig of summer savory
1 oz (30 g/¼ stick) approx. butter
1-2 teasp. summer savory, freshly
   chopped
sea salt and freshly ground pepper

Serves 8

Bring the water to a rolling boil, add the sea salt, broad beans and a sprig of savory. Continue to boil very fast for 3-4 minutes or until just cooked. Drain immediately. Melt the butter in the saucepan, toss in the broad beans and season with freshly ground pepper. Taste, add some more savory and a little sea salt if necessary.

* Broad Beans with Bacon

1 lb (450 g) shelled broad beans
sprig of summer savory
    (optional)
1 tablesp. approx. olive oil
2 ozs (55 g) streaky bacon, cut
    into ¼ inch (5 mm) lardons
2 tablesp. approx. chopped spring
    onion *or* scallion
½ pint (300 ml/1¼ cups) creamy
    milk
roux (see glossary)
salt and freshly ground pepper

Garnish
1-2 tablesp. chopped parsley

Serves 4-6

C ook the broad beans with the savory in well salted boiling water until just tender – 3-5 minutes.

Drain.
Meanwhile heat the olive oil in a frying pan and cook the lardons of bacon until crisp. Add the spring onion or scallion and sweat gently for a few minutes. Add the milk and bring to the boil, thicken with roux to a light coating consistency, and season with salt and freshly ground pepper. Add the broad beans and parsley. Allow to bubble up and heat through. Taste and correct the seasoning. Pour into a hot dish and serve scattered with freshly snipped parsley.

    Note: A crust of buttered crumbs mixed with Cheddar cheese makes this a substantial supper dish; we have also enjoyed it as a sauce for spaghetti with a little marjoram added also.

Pasta with Broad Beans, Pancetta and Olive Oil

T *his is a favourite Sicilian peasant lunchtime dish during the broad bean season.*

1 lb (450 g) pasta (we use
    spaghetti)
3 tablesp. approx. olive oil
4 ozs (110 g) pancetta or mild
    very thinly sliced streaky
    bacon
3 cloves of garlic, crushed
1 lb (450 g) broad beans, shelled,
    blanched and refreshed

1-2 tablesp. approx. freshly
    chopped parsley
freshly grated Parmesan cheese
    (Parmigiano Reggiano if
    possible)

Serves 4

Cook the pasta in boiling salted water. When it is almost cooked, heat the oil in a frying pan, add the pancetta or diced bacon and cook until crispish; add the garlic, cook for a minute or so, then add the broad beans and parsley.

When the pasta is just cooked, drain immediately, toss in a little butter and olive oil and mix with the broad beans and pancetta. Sprinkle with some freshly grated Parmesan cheese and serve immediately.

Beans, French and Runner

I think it is a great shame that so many restaurants serve French beans ad nauseam the whole year round, usually undercooked, with the result that people are bored to death with them. Like so many other vegetables, they should be enjoyed during their short season – and the marvellous thing is that they *can* be eaten at every stage of their development, from the time that they are as slender as the tines of a fork right through to the final stage, when the beans swell in the pods. They can be harvested and cooked as flageolets, and if you let them dry you will have haricot beans for winter stews and casseroles.

From the gardener's point of view there are myriad different varieties including the beautiful speckled Barlottis, golden-podded Tuscan beans and purple French beans. To tell the truth, these are a bit of a swizz because they lose their colour in the cooking, but they can look wonderful in the garden.

We mustn't forget the oldfashioned Scarlet Runner beans which I grow every year, partly because they look so irresistible growing up the beanpoles and tumbling over trellises. The recipes for French beans can be used for runner beans provided that you put them through a bean slicer. You may find you already have one in your kitchen drawer – at the end of your swiveltop peeler.

ᵛ* French Beans

I have found that French beans need a lot of salt in the cooking water to bring up the flavour. They don't benefit from being kept in a hostess trolley, so if you need to cook them ahead try the method I suggest here. I think it works very well.

2 lbs (900 g) French beans
2 pints (1.1 L/5 cups) water
2 teasp. sea salt
1-2 ozs (30-55 g/¼-½ stick)
**   butter**
sea salt and freshly ground pepper

Serves 8

Top and tail the beans. If they are small and thin leave them whole; if they are larger cut them into 1-1½ inch (2.5-4 cm) pieces at an angle.

Bring the water to a fast rolling boil, add 2 teaspoons of salt, then toss in the beans. Continue to boil very fast for 5-6 minutes or until just cooked (they should retain a little bite). Drain immediately.* Melt the butter in the saucepan, toss the beans in it, taste, and season with freshly ground pepper and a little sea salt if necessary.

*The beans may be refreshed under cold water at this point, drained and kept aside for several hours.

To reheat precooked beans: Just before serving, plunge them into boiling salted water for 30 seconds to 1 minute, drain and toss in butter. Correct the seasoning and serve immediately.

ᵛᵛ French Beans with Fresh Chilli

When the beans are cooked, drain well. Heat 2 tablespoons approx. of olive oil in a wide sauté pan, add 1 chopped clove of garlic and 1-2 chopped chillies, toss; season well with sea salt and freshly ground pepper, and add 1 tablespoon of coarsely chopped parsley. Toss, taste and serve.

ᵛ Runner Beans

Top, tail, string and slice the beans and cook as for French beans.

ᵛᵛ French Beans with Tomato Fondue

Cook the French beans as in the master recipe and drain them. Mix with 1 quantity of the recipe for Tomato Fondue (see below). Heat through and serve.

vv Tomato Fondue

2 lbs (900 g) very ripe tomatoes *or*
    ½ fresh and ½ tinned
4 ozs (110 g/1 cup) sliced onion
1 clove of garlic, crushed
    (optional)
1 dessertsp. olive oil
salt, freshly ground pepper and
    sugar to taste
1 tablesp. approx. of any of the
    following, chopped: thyme,
    parsley, mint, basil, lemon
    balm, marjoram

Serves 6 approx.

S weat the sliced onion and garlic (if used) in oil on a gentle heat. It is vital for the success of this dish that the onion is completely soft before the tomatoes are added. Remove the hard core from the tomatoes. Put them into a deep bowl and cover with boiling water.

Count to 10, then pour off the water immediately; peel off the skins, slice the tomatoes and add to the onion. Season with salt, freshly ground pepper and sugar and add a generous sprinkling of chopped herbs. Cook for 10-20 minutes more, or until the tomatoes soften.

Note: Tinned tomatoes need more sugar than fresh.

vv Italian Marinated Bean Salad

M *arcella Hazan introduced me to this sensational bean and herb salad.*

1 lb (450 g) green French beans *or*
    a mixture of green and yellow
    beans
2 tablesp. approx. chopped
    parsley
8-10 fresh basil leaves, chopped
1 teaspoon chopped annual
    marjoram (oregano)
5 tablesp. (7 American tablesp.)
    wine vinegar
2 tablesp. (2½ American tablesp.)
    onion, very finely chopped
2 cloves of garlic, crushed
4 tablesp. (5 American tablesp.)
    extra virgin olive oil
sea salt and freshly ground black
    pepper

Serves 4-6

Mix the parsley, basil, oregano and wine vinegar in a bowl, then add the onion and garlic, mix and let steep for at least 30 minutes.

Meanwhile prepare the beans; cut in half and cook in boiling salted water (see page 14) until *al dente*. Drain and toss in the marinade while still hot. Leave for at least 1 hour to marinate.

Add the olive oil and season with sea salt and freshly ground black pepper, saving a little olive oil to drizzle over the salad just before serving. Best at room temperature.

vv* Salad of Fresh and Dried Beans with Toasted Hazelnuts and Coriander

Dried peas, beans and pulses are a very valuable and inexpensive source of protein, particularly important for vegetarians. In this salad they are attractively combined with freshly cooked French beans. The secret is to toss all the beans in the well flavoured dressing while they are still warm. Each has its own particular flavour so experiment with different combinations. Chick peas are also excellent.

1 lb (450 g) French beans
¼ lb (110 g/¾ cup) haricot beans
¼ lb (110 g/¾ cup) red kidney beans
¼ lb (110 g/¾ cup) flageolet beans
¼ lb (110 g/¾ cup) black-eye beans
a few carrots, onions + bouquet garni
4 tablesp. (5 American tablesp.) well seasoned French Dressing (see page 42)
2 tablesp. chopped parsley
2 tablesp. chopped fresh coriander

sea salt and freshly ground pepper
3-4 ozs (85-110 g/¾ cup) toasted hazelnuts, roughly chopped

Garnish
coarsely chopped coriander

Serves 8

Soak the various types of dried beans separately in cold water overnight.

Next day cover with fresh water, each in a separate saucepan. Add a little carrot, onion and bouquet garni to each and cook until just tender. Drain and reserve the nutritious cooking water for soup.

Cook the French beans (see page 14) and drain them.

Toss all the beans in well flavoured French dressing while still warm, add the parsley and coriander, then season well with sea salt and freshly ground pepper.

Scatter with chopped toasted hazelnuts and garnish with coriander.

vv* Spicy Green Beans

Every guest cook who comes to the Ballymaloe Cookery School introduces us to a few treasures which we incorporate into our repertoire. Madhur Jaffrey, whose recipe this is, has contributed more than most. I would recommend her books to all those who would like to add a little spice to their lives. Spicy Green Beans are delicious either warm or cold, and even better a few days later. Serve as a starter, vegetable or salad.

Asparagus with Hollandaise Sauce

Justin's Aubergine and Mozzarella Sandwich

Oldfashioned Salad with Shanagarry Cream Dressing

Aubergines with Various Toppings

Roast Stuffed Duck with Red Cabbage

1½ lb (675 g) French beans
a piece of fresh ginger, 1½ x 1 in
    (4 x 2.5 cm) approx., peeled
    and coarsely chopped
10 cloves of garlic
10 fl oz (300 ml/1¼ cups) water
5 tablesp. (7 American tablesp.)
    olive oil
2 teasp. whole cumin seeds
1 whole, dried hot red chilli,
    lightly crushed in a mortar
2 teasp. ground coriander seeds
½ lb (225 g) very ripe tomatoes,*
    peeled and finely chopped
1¼ teasp. approx. salt
3 tablesp. approx. freshly
    squeezed lemon juice *or* to
    taste
1 teasp. ground roasted cumin
    seeds (see below)
freshly ground black pepper

Serves 6

Trim the beans and cut them
crosswise at 1 inch (2.5 cm) intervals.
Put the ginger and garlic into the
container of an electric blender or
food processor. Add 4 fl oz (120 ml/
½ cup) of the measured water and
blend until fairly smooth.

Heat the oil in a wide, heavy
saucepan over a medium flame.
When hot, put in the cumin seeds.
Five seconds later, put in the crushed
chilli. As soon as it darkens, pour in
the ginger-garlic paste. Stir and cook
for 1 minute approx. Add the
coriander and stir a few times. Now
put in the chopped tomatoes, stir and
cook for 2 minutes approx., mashing
up the tomato pieces with the back of
a slotted spoon as you do so.

Put in the beans, salt and the
remaining water. Bring to simmering
point. Cover, turn the heat to low
and cook for 8-10 minutes approx. or
until the beans are tender.

Remove the cover. Add the
lemon juice, roasted cumin and a
generous amount of freshly ground
pepper. Turn the heat up and boil
away virtually all of the liquid,
stirring the beans gently as you do so.

*If you are using tinned tomatoes
add 1 teaspoon of sugar to the recipe.

Beetroot

I blame those glass jars of bitter pickled beetroot for putting so many people off a vegetable which has far more exciting possibilities. It deserves a better fate!

Beetroot is terrifically versatile and the great bonus is that if you grow it yourself (and it's certainly not difficult) then you can enjoy it from the time the beets are walnut-sized until they are fully grown. Don't just boil it all the time. Try it baked, or grated and quickly sautéed in butter, or cut into fine strips and deepfried until crispy, then scattered on a salad. Indeed, beetroot leaves can be used in salads or in soups.

In America beetroot is now being hailed as the great new wonder food for reducing cholesterol!

vv* How to cook beetroot

Leave 2 inches (5 cm) of leaf stalks on top and the whole root on the beet. Hold it under a running tap and wash off the mud with the palms of your hands, so that you don't damage the skin; otherwise the beetroot will bleed during cooking. Cover with cold water and add a little salt and sugar. Cover the pot, bring to the boil and simmer either on top or in the oven, for 1-2 hours depending on size. It is done if the skin rubs off easily and if it dents when pressed with a finger.

vv Pickled Beetroot and Onion Salad

1 lb (450 g) cooked beetroot
8 ozs (225 g/1 cup) sugar
16 fl ozs (475 ml/2 cups) water

1 onion, peeled and thinly sliced (optional)
8 fl ozs (250 ml/1 cup) white wine vinegar

Serves 5-6

Dissolve the sugar in water and bring to the boil. Add the sliced onion and simmer for 3-4 minutes. Add the

vinegar, pour over the peeled sliced beets and leave to cool.

Note: The onion may be omitted if desired.

^{v*} Baked Beetroot

T*his method of cooking beetroot, though slower than boiling, gives a deliciously sweet and intense flavour. The beets are particularly good hot.*

4 medium-sized beetroot
sea salt and butter
chopped parsley (optional)

Serves 4

Wash each beetroot gently, keeping both the root and stalk end intact.

Wrap each beet in a loose tinfoil parcel and bake in a preheated oven, 200°C/400°F/regulo 6, for 1 hour approx., by which time the skin will rub off easily and the flavour will be rich, intense and deliciously earthy.

Eat with a little butter and sea salt, and a little chopped parsley if desired.

^v Baby Beets with Lemon and Fresh Herbs

T*he great bonus of growing your own beets is that you can harvest them when they are even smaller than golf balls – tender, sweet and delicious. At that stage they make an irresistible vegetable, particularly good with roast beef, duck or goose.*

18-24 baby beetroots
1 oz (30 g/¼ stick) approx. butter
freshly squeezed lemon juice
sea salt, freshly ground pepper
    and sugar
freshly chopped herbs

Trim the leaves 1-2 inches (2.5-5 cm) above the root and do not cut the tail. Wash the beetroot gently under cold water, rub off any clay with your hands but do not scrub because this could damage the skins and the beetroot would bleed during cooking. Boil for 15-20 minutes depending on size.

Peel off the skins. Melt the butter in a saucepan and toss the beetroots in it. Sharpen with lemon juice, season with sea salt, freshly ground pepper and sugar, sprinkle with herbs and serve immediately.

A little cream added at this stage is also delicious.

^v Oldfashioned Salad with Shanagarry Cream Dressing

*T*his simple, oldfashioned salad is one
of my absolute favourites. It's quite
delicious when made with crisp lettuce,
good home-grown Irish tomatoes and
cucumbers, free-range eggs and home-
preserved beetroot. On the other hand, if
you make it with pale battery eggs, watery
tomatoes, tired lettuce and cucumber and –
worst of all – vinegary beetroot from a jar,
you'll wonder why you bothered!

We serve this traditional salad in
Ballymaloe as a starter, with an
oldfashioned salad dressing which would
have been popular before the days of
mayonnaise.

2 hardboiled eggs, quartered
4 slices of home-preserved
    beetroot
1 butterhead lettuce (the ordinary
    lettuce on sale everywhere)
4 tiny scallions *or* spring onions
2-4 firm, ripe tomatoes,
    quartered
16 thin slices of cucumber
2-4 radishes, sliced
chopped parsley

^v SHANAGARRY CREAM DRESSING

2 hardboiled eggs
1 level teasp. dry mustard
pinch of salt
1 tablesp. (1 American tablesp. +
    1 teasp.) soft brown sugar
1 tablesp. (1 American tablesp. +
    1 teasp.) brown malt vinegar
2-4 fl ozs (60-120 ml/¼- ½ cup)
    cream

Garnish
spring onion
watercress
chopped parsley

Serves 4

*T*o hardboil the eggs for the salad
and the dressing, bring a small
saucepan of water to the boil, gently
slide in the eggs, boil for 10 minutes
(12 if they are very fresh), strain off
the hot water and cover with cold
water. Peel when cold.

Wash and dry the lettuce and
scallions.

Next make the dressing. Cut
2 eggs in half, sieve the yolks into a
bowl, add the mustard, sugar and salt.
Blend in the vinegar and cream.
Chop the egg whites and add some to
the sauce. Keep the rest to scatter
over the salad. Cover the dressing
until needed.

To assemble the salads: Arrange a
few lettuce leaves on each of 4 plates.
Scatter a few pieces of tomato and
2 hardboiled egg quarters, a few slices

of cucumber, 1 radish and 2 slices of beetroot on each plate. Garnish with spring onion and watercress, scatter the remaining chopped egg white (from the dressing) over the salad and some chopped parsley.

Put a tiny bowl of the dressing in the centre of each plate and serve immediately while the salad is crisp and before the beetroot starts to run. Alternatively, the dressing may be served from one large bowl.

^v Beetroot Relish

This sweet-sour relish is particularly good with cold meats and coarse country terrines, e.g. Pork, Spinach and Herb Terrine (see page 115).

1 lb (450 g) beetroot, peeled and grated
8 ozs (225 g) onion, chopped
1½ ozs (45 g/⅜ stick) butter
3 tablesp. (4 American tablesp.) sugar
salt and freshly ground pepper

1 fl oz (30 ml) sherry vinegar
4 fl ozs (120 ml/½ cup) red wine
2 teasp. grated fresh ginger

Sweat the onion slowly in butter until very soft, add the sugar and seasoning and allow to brown slightly. Add the rest of the ingredients and cook gently for 30 minutes. Serve cold.

This relish keeps for ages.

^v Beetroot, Potato and Parsley Purée

This is particularly good with venison, pheasant or duck.

8 ozs (225 g) freshly mashed potato
4 fl ozs (120 ml/½ cup) creamy milk, approx.
10 ozs (285 g) beetroot, freshly cooked, peeled and grated
1 tablesp. freshly chopped parsley
salt and freshly ground pepper
1 oz (30 g/¼ stick) butter

Serves 4

Heat the milk to boiling point. Mix it into freshly mashed potato, add the grated beetroot, chopped parsley and butter, season with salt and freshly ground pepper, and mix thoroughly. Taste and correct the seasoning. Serve hot.

Broccoli or Calabrese

v* *How to cook green broccoli or calabrese*
v *Broccoli with Butter and Lemon*
vv *Calabrese with Chilli and Garlic*
v *Pizza with Broccoli, Mozzarella and Garlic Slivers*
Gratin of Broccoli and Chicken

This vegetable, sadly overexposed and often overcooked, is in fact part of a large and exciting family which includes the great winter standbys, white and purple sprouting broccoli, and a marvellous old Irish vegetable which I came across only recently in the gardens of Glin Castle. Since I have begun to grow it myself, several people have recognised it as a forgotten part of their childhood and given it different names – Winter Kale, Winter Greens, Cut and Come, Hungry Gap. It produces greens right through the winter when there is very little else in the garden.

If you don't grow your own broccoli, it can be a ferociously expensive vegetable unless you know about peeling the thick stalk as described below. But remember, broccoli doesn't always have to be cooked. If it is very fresh and crisp, the little florets are particularly good in a winter or green salad with a robust dressing.

v* How to cook green broccoli or calabrese

The secret of real flavour in broccoli, as in so many other green vegetables, is not just freshness. It needs to be cooked in well salted water. If you grow your own, cut out the central head but leave the plant intact, and very soon you'll have lots of smaller florets.

1 lb (450 g) sprouting broccoli (green, purple *or* white) *or* calabrese
1 pint (600 ml/2½ cups) water
1½ teasp. salt
butter
lots of freshly ground pepper

Serves 4

Peel the stems with a knife or potato peeler, cut off the stalk close to the head and cut into ½ inch (1 cm) pieces. If the heads are large divide the florets into small clusters.

Add the salt to the water, bring to a fast boil, first add the stalks and then the florets, and cook uncovered at a rolling boil for 5-6 minutes. Drain off the water while the broccoli still has a bite.*

Taste, season with freshly ground pepper and serve immediately.

Better still, melt a little butter in a saucepan until it foams, toss the broccoli gently in it, season to taste and serve immediately.

*Broccoli can be blanched and refreshed earlier in the day and then reheated in a saucepan of boiling salted water just before serving.

ᵛ Broccoli with Butter and Lemon

Cook the broccoli until *al dente* as above.

Melt 1 oz (30 g/¼ stick) butter in a saucepan, add the juice of a lemon, and toss the broccoli in it gently. Season with lots of freshly ground pepper and serve immediately.

ᵛᵛ Calabrese with Chilli and Garlic

Cook the calabrese until *al dente* as above.

Heat 3 tablespoons approx. of olive oil in a saucepan, add 1-2 chopped cloves of garlic, and 1 chopped and deseeded chilli. Allow to sizzle for 1-2 minutes, pour over the hot calabrese and toss gently. Serve immediately.

ᵛ Pizza with Broccoli, Mozzarella and Garlic Slivers

This is one of my favourite pizzas, originally made for me by an American student, Erin Thomas.

4 ozs (110 g) calabrese *or* green broccoli
7 ozs (200 g) olive oil dough (see below – I make 1 quantity of the recipe and use ⅙ of the dough for each pizza)

2 tablesp. (2½ American tablesp.) olive oil
2-3 cloves of garlic, cut into thin slivers
3 ozs (85 g) grated Mozzarella cheese (di Bufala if possible)
½ oz (15 g) grated Parmesan cheese, preferably Parmigiano Reggiano (optional)
extra virgin olive oil
sea salt

Makes 1, serves 1-2

Cook the broccoli florets in boiling salted water (see page 23) until *al dente*.

Preheat the oven to 250°C/ 475°F/regulo 9.

Roll out the dough as thinly as possible into a round 10-12 inches (25.5-30.5 cm) in diameter. Sprinkle some semolina on to the pizza paddle and place the dough on top. Brush the surface of the dough with olive oil. Sprinkle on the slivers of garlic, arrange the broccoli on top and sprinkle with Mozzarella cheese and a little Parmesan cheese if you like.

Drizzle with olive oil and season with sea salt. Slide off the paddle on to a hot baking sheet in the fully preheated oven. Bake for 10-12 minutes and serve immediately.

vv* Olive Oil Dough for Pizza

I n my family everyone loves pizza but each one has his or her own particular favourite. I usually divide the dough into 6 pieces and then I can use lots of different toppings and keep everybody happy.

1½ lbs (675 g/5¼ cups) strong
　white flour
½ oz (15 g/1 American tablesp. +
　1 teasp.) sugar
¾ oz (20 g) fresh yeast *or* half the
　quantity of dried yeast
¾ pint (450 ml/scant 2 cups)
　lukewarm water – more if
　needed
2-4 tablesp. (2½-5 American
　tablesp.) olive oil
2 level teasp. (1 American teasp.)
　salt

Mix the sugar and yeast with ¼ pint (150 ml/¾ cup) of the lukewarm water, stir and leave for a few minutes until dissolved. Add the olive oil and the remainder of the water. Sieve the flour and salt into a bowl, make a well in the centre and pour in most of the lukewarm liquid. Mix to a loose dough adding the remainder of the liquid or more flour if necessary. Turn the dough on to a floured board, cover and leave to relax for 5 minutes. Then knead for 10 minutes approx. or until smooth and springy (if kneading in a food mixer with a dough hook, 5 minutes is usually long enough).

Put the dough to rise in a pottery or delph bowl and cover the top of the bowl tightly with cling film. Yeast dough rises best in a warm moist atmosphere, e.g. near your cooker, on top of a radiator or in a fan oven turned to minimum heat with the door left ajar. Rising time depends on the temperature – in an average kitchen it will take 2-3 hours.

When the dough has well doubled in size, knead again for approx. 2-3 minutes until all the air has been forced out again – this is called 'knocking back'. Leave to relax again for 10 minutes and then use the dough as you choose. I find it very convenient to pop a few rolled out uncooked pizza bases into the freezer. You can take one out, put the topping on and slide it straight into the oven. What could be simpler!

This dough also makes delicious white yeast bread which we shape into rolls, loaves and plaits.

Gratin of Broccoli and Chicken

T his is one of those dishes that can be mouth-watering or a complete disaster. Its success depends on the broccoli being carefully cooked so that it is bright green and just tender.

1 × 3½ lb (1.5 kg) chicken,
    free-range if possible
1 lb (450 g) broccoli florets
2 carrots, sliced
2 onions, sliced
sprig each of thyme and tarragon
a few peppercorns
½ pint (300 ml/1¼ cup)
    homemade chicken stock
4 ozs (110 g/2 cups) mushrooms,
    sliced
scrap of butter
6 fl ozs (175 ml/¾ cup) milk
¼ pint (150 ml/generous ½ cup)
    cream
2 teasp. chopped tarragon *or*
    annual marjoram
roux (see glossary)
1 oz (30 g/½ cup) Buttered
    Crumbs (see page 65)
1 oz (30 g/¼ cup) grated Cheddar
    cheese

lasagne dish, 10 × 8 inches (25.5 ×
    20.5 cm)

Serves 4-6

Put the chicken into a saucepan or casserole with the onions and carrots, add thyme, tarragon and peppercorns. Pour in the stock, bring to the boil, cover and simmer for 1–1¼ hours or until the chicken is tender.

Meanwhile cook the broccoli florets in boiling salted water until *al dente* (see page 23). Drain and refresh under cold water, and keep aside. Sauté the mushrooms in the butter on a hot pan and keep aside also.

When the chicken is cooked remove the meat from one side and carve into bite-sized pieces. Keep the rest for another recipe.

Strain and degrease the cooking liquid, add the milk and cream, bring to the boil, add the tarragon or annual marjoram, simmer for a few minutes, thicken to a light coating consistency with roux, then add the chicken to the sauce. Butter an ovenproof lasagne dish, put a layer of broccoli on the base, scatter the mushrooms on top and cover with the creamy chicken mixture.

Mix the Buttered Crumbs with grated cheese and sprinkle over the surface. Reheat in a moderate oven, 180°C/350°F/regulo 4, for 15–20 minutes and flash under the grill until the top is crunchy and golden. Serve immediately.

Brussels Sprouts

v* How to cook Brussels sprouts
v* Brussels Sprouts with Buttered Almonds
Brussels Sprouts with Buttered Almonds and Bacon

Every time I eat Brussels sprouts I think of the heroic pickers who harvest them in the freezing cold on winter mornings. My husband Timmy, remembering the penance of this from his days at agricultural college, always swore he would never grow them commercially. And after all that effort, three-quarters of the Brussels sprouts that are grown are massacred in the cooking. If this book does nothing else but show people how to cook Brussels sprouts properly, it will be worth it!

Keen gardeners, particularly those who are interested in decorative vegetables, might like to try the purply-wine varieties which look so stunning in a winter garden, especially when they are covered with frost and icicles.

v* How to cook Brussels sprouts

The traditional way to cook Brussels sprouts was to cut a cross in the stalk so that they would, hopefully, cook more evenly. However, I discovered quite by accident when I was in a mad rush one day, that if you cut sprouts in half they cook much faster and taste infinitely more delicious. With this recipe I've managed to convert many ardent Brussels sprouts haters.

1 lb (450 g) Brussels sprouts
1 pint (600 ml/2½ cups) water
1½ teasp. salt

1-2 ozs (30-55 g/¼- ½ stick) butter
salt and freshly ground pepper

Serves 4-6

Choose even, medium-sized sprouts. Trim the outer leaves if necessary and cut them in half lengthwise. Salt the water and bring to a fast rolling boil. Toss in the sprouts, cover the saucepan just for a minute until the water returns to the boil, then uncover and maintain for 5-6 minutes or until the sprouts are cooked through but still have a slight bite. Pour off the water.*

Melt the butter in a saucepan, roll the sprouts gently in the butter, season with lots of freshly ground pepper and salt. Taste and serve immediately in a hot serving dish.

★ If the sprouts are not to be served immediately, refresh them under cold water as soon as they are cooked. Just before serving, drop them into boiling salted water for a few seconds to heat through. Drain and toss in the butter, season and serve. This way they will taste almost as good as if they were freshly cooked: certainly much more delicious than sprouts kept warm for half an hour in an oven or a hostess trolley.

v* Brussels Sprouts with Buttered Almonds

C ook the sprouts in the usual way. Meanwhile melt 1 oz (30 g) butter in a frying pan, toss in 2 ozs (55 g) approx. nibbed almonds and cook for a few minutes or until golden. As soon as the sprouts are cooked, drain and toss with the buttered almonds. Serve immediately in a hot dish.

Brussels Sprouts with Buttered Almonds and Bacon

A dd 2-4 ozs (55-110 g) of crispy bacon lardons to the above recipe and serve immediately.

Cabbage

^v Boiled Cabbage
^v Buttered Cabbage
^{v*} Coleslaw
^{vv} Cabbage Salad with Raisins and Mint
^v Colcannon
Traditional Irish Bacon, Cabbage and Parsley Sauce
^{*vv} Chinese Seaweed – Deepfried Cabbage
Warm Red Cabbage Salad with Bacon, Croûtons and Irish Blue Cheese
[*] Roast Stuffed Duck with Apple Sauce and Red Cabbage

Another of my many crusades is to reinstate cabbage, the most traditional of Irish vegetables, as something to cook and serve with pride. It's time we all put the memory of grim school dinner cabbage behind us! In the boarding school where I was educated as a young lady, we flushed so much cabbage down the loo that we managed to block up the drains!

There are certainly a great many more ways of dealing with cabbage than to boil it into oblivion. It's worth remembering that there are different varieties, in season at different times. The soft spring cabbage keeps us going into early summer, the crinkly Savoy sees us through autumn and winter, and now red cabbage livens up hearty winter meals too.

If you grow your own, seek out the frilly ornamental varieties. Although the leaves are tougher, they will give your vegetable garden colour even on the bleakest January days.

^v Boiled Cabbage

The traditional way of cooking cabbage is to boil fairly finely shredded cabbage (stalks removed) in salted water, or better still bacon cooking water, until done. The cooking time varies depending on the variety of cabbage, so keep a watchful eye and drain the cabbage as soon as it is cooked. Add a nice lump of butter, season with lots of freshly ground pepper and a little more salt if necessary.

ᵛ Buttered Cabbage

T his method takes only a few minutes to cook but first the cabbage must be carefully sliced into fine shreds. It should be served the moment it is cooked.

1 lb (450 g) fresh Savoy cabbage
1-2 ozs (30-55 g/¼-½ stick)
butter
salt and freshly ground pepper
a knob of butter

Remove the tough outer leaves from the cabbage. Divide into four, cut out the stalks and then cut into fine shreds across the grain. Put 2-3 tablespoons of water into a wide saucepan with the butter and a pinch of salt. Bring to the boil, add the cabbage and toss constantly over a high heat, then cover for a few minutes. Toss again and add some more salt, freshly ground pepper and a knob of butter. Serve immediately.

ᵛ* Coleslaw

I t's still the hottest item on all deli counters and fast food restaurant menus! If you are making your own, look out for the sweet Irish-grown Drumhead cabbage.

1 lb (450 g) white cabbage
(Drumhead if possible)
1 onion
1 large carrot
sea salt and freshly ground pepper
¼-½ pint (150-300 ml/½-1 cup)
homemade Mayonnaise
(see page 30) or Mayonnaise
and natural yoghurt mixed
1 tablesp. approx. chopped
parsley

Slice the cabbage and onion very thinly either by hand or with a machine. Grate the carrots on the coarsest part of a grater. Mix with the cabbage and onion, season with salt and freshly ground pepper. Fold in the Mayonnaise or Mayonnaise and yoghurt. Taste and correct the seasoning. Sprinkle with chopped parsley and serve immediately or keep refrigerated.

VARIATIONS
Add some diced or finely sliced celery stalks, or 1 crisp eating apple tossed in 2 tablespoons of lemon juice, or 2 ozs (55 g/scant ½ cup) of sultanas and 1 tablespoon of freshly chopped mint.

ᵛ MAYONNAISE

Mayonnaise is what we call a 'mother sauce' in culinary jargon. In fact it is the 'mother' of all the cold emulsion sauces, so once you can make mayonnaise you can make any of the daughter sauces by just adding some extra ingredients.

I know it's very tempting to reach for the jar of 'well-known brand', but most people don't seem to be aware that mayonnaise can be made, even with a hand whisk, in under 5 minutes; and if you use a food processor the technique is still the same but it's made in just a couple of minutes. The great secret is to have all your ingredients at room temperature and to drip the oil very slowly into the egg yolks at the beginning. The quality of your mayonnaise will depend totally on the quality of your egg yolks, oil and vinegar and it's perfectly possible to make a bland mayonnaise if you use poor quality ingredients.

2 egg yolks, preferably free-range
¼ teasp. salt
pinch of English mustard *or* ¼ teasp. French mustard
15 ml/1 dessertsp. white wine vinegar
8 fl ozs (250 ml/1 cup) oil (sunflower, arachide *or* olive oil, *or* a mixture)

Serve with cold cooked meats, fowl, fish, eggs and vegetables.

Put the egg yolks into a bowl with the mustard, salt and 1 dessertspoon of the wine vinegar (keep the whites to make meringues). Put the oil into a measure. Take a whisk in one hand and the oil in the other and drip the oil on to the egg yolks, drop by drop, whisking at the same time. Within a minute you will notice that the mixture is beginning to thicken. When this happens you can add the oil a little faster, but don't get too cheeky or it will suddenly curdle because the egg yolks can only absorb the oil at a certain pace. When all the oil has been added, taste and add a little more seasoning if necessary.

If the mayonnaise curdles it will suddenly become quite thin, and, if left sitting, the oil will start to float to the top of the sauce. If this happens you can quite easily rectify the situation by putting another egg yolk or 1-2 tablespoons of boiling water into a clean bowl, then whisking in the curdled mayonnaise, a half teaspoon at a time, until it emulsifies again.

ᵛᵛ Cabbage Salad with Raisins and Mint

*I*f you are tiring of the ubiquitous coleslaw, then you might like to try this fresh-tasting cabbage salad.

¼ **white cabbage with a good heart**
1 **large dessert apple, grated**
1 **tablesp. approx. raisins**
1 **dessertsp. chopped mint**
1 **dessertsp. chopped chives**
2 **tablesp. approx. pure Irish honey**
2 **teasp. white wine vinegar**

Cut the cabbage in quarters. Wash it well and discard the coarse outer leaves. Cut away the stalks and shred the heart very finely with a sharp knife. Put it into a bowl with the other ingredients, except for the honey and vinegar which should be mixed together. Toss the salad in the dressing until well coated. Taste and correct the seasoning, and serve soon.

ᵛ Colcannon

*T*his traditional Irish potato dish, comfort food at its very best, has now been 'discovered' and often features on smart restaurant menus in London and New York. Sadly, despite my best efforts to encourage Irish people to have pride in their traditional dishes, it is not yet popular on restaurant menus at home!

1 **lb (450 g) Savoy *or* spring cabbage**
2½-3 **lbs (1.15-1.4 kg) 'old' potatoes – Golden Wonders *or* Kerr's Pinks**
8 **fl ozs (250 ml/1 cup) approx. boiling milk**
4 **ozs (110 g) scallion *or* spring onion**
salt and freshly ground pepper
2 **ozs (55 g/½ stick) approx. butter**

Serves 8 approx.

Scrub the potatoes, put them in a saucepan of cold water, add a good pinch of salt and bring to the boil. When the potatoes are about half cooked (15 minutes approx. for 'old' potatoes), strain off two-thirds of the water, replace the lid on the saucepan, put on to a gentle heat and allow the potatoes to steam until they are cooked.

Remove the dark outer leaves from the cabbage. Wash the rest and cut into quarters, remove the core and cut finely into shreds across the grain. Boil in a little boiling salted water or bacon cooking water until soft. Drain, season with salt, freshly ground pepper and a little butter.

When the potatoes are just cooked, put the milk and the finely chopped scallion into a saucepan and bring to the boil. Pull the peel off the potatoes and discard, mash quickly while they are still warm and beat in enough of the boiling milk to make a fluffy purée. (If you have a large quantity, put the potatoes in the bowl of a food mixer and beat with the spade.) Then stir in the cooked cabbage and taste for seasoning.

For perfection, serve immediately in a hot dish with a lump of butter melting in the centre.

Colcannon may be prepared ahead up to this point and reheated later in a moderate oven, 180°C/350°F/regulo 4, for 20-25 minutes approx. Cover while reheating so it doesn't get too crusty on top.

Traditional Irish Bacon, Cabbage and Parsley Sauce

Our national dish of bacon and cabbage is often a sorry disappointment nowadays, partly because it is so difficult to get good quality bacon with a decent bit of fat on it. The Strawberry Tree in Killarney is one of the few Irish restaurants that offers our national dish proudly. I was served Bacon and Cabbage there in a particularly novel and delicious way.

4-5 lbs (1.8-2.25 kg) loin of bacon, either smoked *or* unsmoked (with the rind on and a nice covering of fat)
Buttered *or* Boiled Cabbage (see pages 28, 29)
Parsley Sauce (see below)

Cover the bacon in cold water and bring slowly to the boil. If the bacon is very salty there will be a white froth on top of the water, in which case it is preferable to discard the water and start again. It may be

necessary to change the water several times depending on how salty the bacon is. Finally cover with hot water and simmer until almost cooked, allowing 20 minutes to the pound. Remove the rind and serve with Buttered or Boiled Cabbage and Parsley Sauce.

Note: We use loin of bacon off the bone. I find the bacon I get from McCarrons of Cavan to be sweet and succulent. And while I am on the subject of bacon, the best smoky rashers I know of come from Noreen Curran's butcher shop in Dingle.

Parsley Sauce
1 pint (600 ml/2½ cups) milk
2 ozs (55 g) roux (see glossary)
salt and freshly ground pepper
a few slices of carrot ⎫
a few slices of onion ⎬ optional
bouquet garni ⎭
chopped parsley

If using herbs and vegetables, put them in the cold milk and bring to simmering point, season and simmer for 4-5 minutes. Strain out the herbs and vegetables, bring the milk back to the boil, and whisk in the roux until the sauce is a light coating consistency. Season with salt and freshly ground pepper. Add chopped parsley and simmer on a very low heat for 4-5 minutes.

vv* Chinese Seaweed – Deepfried Cabbage

Surprisingly, the Chinese seaweed served in many Chinese restaurants has nothing to do with seaweed – it is merely deepfried cabbage. This original way of cooking cabbage tastes absolutely delicious and becomes addictive once you start to eat it – just like peanuts or popcorn!

**Savoy *or* spring green cabbage
salt
sugar**

Remove the stalks from the outer leaves. Roll the dry leaves into a cigar shape and slice with a very sharp knife into the finest possible shreds.

Heat the oil in a deepfrier to 180°C/350°F. Toss in some of the cabbage and cook for a few seconds. As soon as it starts to crisp, remove and drain on kitchen paper. Sprinkle with salt and sugar, toss and serve cold.

Warm Red Cabbage Salad with Bacon, Croûtons and Irish Blue Cheese

A robust winter salad which can be served as a starter or main course.

**1 lb (450 g) red cabbage
4 tablesp. approx. wine vinegar
olive oil for frying
18 little croûtons cut from a thin
    French stick
8 ozs (225 g) streaky bacon, diced
    into ¼ inch (5 mm) lardons
3 ozs (85 g) Irish Blue Cheese –
    Cashel Blue, Chetwynd *or*
    Abbey Blue Brie**

Dressing
**3 tablesp. wine vinegar
9 tablesp. olive oil
1 teasp. Dijon mustard
1 teasp. Irish whole grain mustard
1 teasp. pure Irish honey
1 clove of garlic, crushed
salt and freshly ground pepper
lettuce leaves – green lollo *or*
    oakleaf**

Garnish
sprigs of chervil *or* flat parsley

Serves 6

Slice the red cabbage very thinly with a sharp knife. Bring the wine vinegar to the boil, pour it over the shredded cabbage in a bowl and toss. The cabbage will turn bright red. Keep aside.

Blanch and refresh the bacon to draw out the excess salt, drain and dry on kitchen paper. Heat ¾ inch (2 cm) approx. of olive oil in a frying pan, and cook the croûtons for a few seconds on each side; when they are pale golden, whip them out and drain on kitchen paper. Strain the oil and save to use for another purpose.

Whisk together all the ingredients for the dressing.

To serve: Arrange a few lettuce leaves on a plate or plates. Heat a little olive oil in the frying pan and cook the lardons until crisp and golden. Meanwhile add 2 ozs (55g/ ½ cup) of crumbled cheese to the red cabbage, toss and mix with enough dressing to make the salad glisten. Pile the cabbage salad into the centre of the plate or plates. Sprinkle the hot lardons and the remainder of the blue cheese over the top. Garnish with the hot croûtons and serve immediately, sprinkled with a few sprigs of chervil or flat parsley.

* Roast Stuffed Duck with Apple Sauce and Red Cabbage

R ed cabbage goes particularly well with roast goose, duck or pork with crackling.

1 free-range duck, 4 lbs (1.8 kg) approx.

Stuffing
3 ozs (85 g/¾ cup) onion, finely chopped
1½ ozs (45 g/⅜ stick) butter
3½ ozs (100 g/1½ cups) soft white breadcrumbs
1 tablesp. approx. freshly chopped sage
salt and freshly ground pepper

Stock
neck and giblets from duck
1 onion
1 carrot, sliced
bouquet garni
2-3 peppercorns

Apple Sauce
1 lb (450 g) cooking apples (Bramley Seedling)
2 ozs (55 g/⅓ cup) sugar approx. (depending on tartness of the apples)
1-2 dessertsp. water

Red Cabbage
see below

Serves 4

To make the stock, put the neck, gizzard, heart and any other trimmings into a saucepan with the carrot cut in slices and the onion cut in quarters. Add a bouquet garni of parsley stalks, small stalk of celery and a sprig of thyme. Cover with cold water and add the peppercorns but no salt.

Bring slowly to the boil and simmer for 2-3 hours. This will make a delicious stock which will be the basis of the gravy. Meanwhile, singe the duck and make the stuffing.

To make the stuffing, sweat the onion in the butter on a gentle heat for 5-10 minutes until soft but not coloured, add the breadcrumbs and sage. Season with salt and pepper to taste. Unless you plan to cook the duck immediately, allow the stuffing to get cold.

When the stuffing is quite cold, season the cavity of the duck and spoon in the stuffing. Roast in a moderate oven, 180°C/350°F/regulo 4, for 1¼ hours approx. When the duck is cooked, remove to a serving dish and allow to rest while you make the gravy.

Degrease the cooking juices (keep the duck fat for roast or sautéed potatoes). Add stock to the juices in the roasting pan, bring to the boil, taste and season if necessary. Strain the gravy into a sauceboat and serve with the duck.

APPLE SAUCE
Peel, quarter and core the apples, cut the quarters in two and put in to a stainless steel or cast iron saucepan,

with the sugar and water. Cover and put over a low heat. As soon as the apple has broken down, stir and taste for sweetness. Serve warm with the duck, red cabbage and gravy.

RED CABBAGE
1 lb (450 g) red cabbage (Red Drummond if possible)
1 lb (450 g) cooking apples (Bramley Seedling)
1 tablesp. approx. wine vinegar
4 fl ozs (120 ml/½ cup) water
1 level teasp. salt
1 heaped tablesp. approx. sugar

Remove any damaged outer leaves from the cabbage. Examine and clean it if necessary. Cut in quarters, remove the core and slice the cabbage finely across the grain. Put the vinegar, water, salt and sugar into a cast iron casserole or stainless steel saucepan. Add the cabbage and bring it to the boil.

Meanwhile, peel and core the apples and cut into quarters (no smaller). Lay them on top of the cabbage, cover and continue to cook gently until the cabbage is tender, 30-50 minutes approx. Do not overcook or the colour and flavour will be ruined. Taste for seasoning and add more sugar if necessary. Serve in a warm serving dish.

Note: Some varieties of red cabbage are quite tough and don't seem to soften much, even with prolonged cooking. Our favourite variety, Red Drummond, gives best results.

Carrots

^v Glazed Carrots
^v Carrot and Mint Soup
^{vv*} Carrot and Apple Salad with Honey
and Vinegar Dressing
^v Carrot and Parsnip, Green, White and Gold or Sunshine
^{v*} Carrot and Potato with Cream and Fresh Spices

We take carrots so utterly for granted that it is difficult to imagine they were once as exotic as salsify is to us now. The ladies of the Stuart court used to pin the feathery foliage in their hats, for sheer style! Now, although they are one of our most common vegetables, they are seldom cooked properly. The secret is to use only a very small amount of water, otherwise all their sweet flavour is lost.

The other secret, of course, is to buy the right carrots! Having tasted the delicious produce of Udo and Penny Lang in Co. Wicklow while we were filming for the television series which this book accompanies, I would urge you to buy organically grown carrots if possible, and Irish-grown carrots at the very least. Buy them with the soil on, because they will both keep and taste better. Above all, never, ever, waste your money on washed, imported carrots in plastic bags or tins, because compared to our home-grown ones they have almost no flavour at all.

For gardeners who are interested in growing their own, carrot fly is the major problem, and it can be a resilient pest, particularly if you are reluctant to spray your crop. The only satisfactory solution is to move your new carrot patch well away from the troublesome old one, and keep moving away for four years at least – difficult in a small garden, obviously.

If you succeed, however, the rewards are substantial. You can try all sorts of different varieties, early and late, and enjoy them at different stages. The thinnings can be eaten as cruditées with dips, and when the carrots are slightly bigger they can be cooked whole, with a little bit of green shoot left on top. Don't forget that the tender green leaves are delicious and nutritious. Include them in your trendy Wilted Greens (see page 69)!

ᵛ Glazed Carrots

You might like to try this method of cooking carrots. Admittedly it takes a little vigilance but the resulting flavour is a revelation to many people.

1 lb (450 g) Irish carrots – Early
    Nantes and Autumn King
    have particularly good flavour
¾ oz (20 g/scant ¼ stick) butter
4 fl ozs (120 ml/½ cup) cold
    water
pinch of salt
good pinch of sugar

Garnish
chopped parsley *or* mint

Serves 4-6

Cut the tops and tips off the carrots, scrub and peel thinly if necessary. Cut into slices ⅓ inch (7 mm) thick, either straight across or at an angle. Leave very young carrots whole.

Put them in a saucepan with the butter, water, salt and sugar. Bring to the boil, cover and cook over a gentle heat until tender, by which time all the liquid should have been absorbed into the carrots; if not, remove the lid and increase the heat until all the water has evaporated. Taste and correct the seasoning. Shake the saucepan so the carrots become coated with the buttery glaze.

Serve in a hot vegetable dish sprinkled with chopped parsley or mint.

ᵛ Carrot and Mint Soup

This soup may be served either hot or cold. Don't hesitate to put in a good pinch of sugar – it brings up the flavour.

1¼ lbs (560 g/4 cups) Irish
    carrots, chopped
1½ ozs (45 g/⅜ stick) butter
4 ozs (110 g/1 cup) onion,
    chopped
5 ozs (140 g/1 cup) potatoes,
    chopped
salt, freshly ground pepper and
    sugar
sprig of mint

2 pints (1.1 L/5 cups) homemade
    light chicken stock
3 teasp. freshly chopped mint
2½ fl ozs (63 ml/generous ½ cup)
    creamy milk (optional)

Garnish
a little whipped cream
sprigs of mint

Serves 6 approx.

Melt the butter and when it foams add the chopped vegetables. Season with salt, freshly ground pepper and sugar. Add the sprig of mint, cover with a butter paper (to retain the steam) and a tight fitting lid. Leave to sweat gently on a low heat for 10 minutes approx. Remove the butter paper, add the stock and boil until the vegetables are soft. Pour into the liquidiser, add the mint and purée until smooth, then taste and adjust seasoning. Add a little creamy milk if necessary.

Garnish with whipped cream and a sprig of fresh mint.

vv* Carrot and Apple Salad with Honey and Vinegar Dressing

T*his delicious salad is very quick to make with ingredients you'd probably have to hand. It can be served as a first course but it is also delicious served as a salad which goes particularly well with ham, bacon or crispy roast pork.*

8 ozs (225 g/2 cups) Irish carrots, grated
10 ozs (285 g/2 cups) dessert apples (e.g. Cox's Orange Pippins if available), grated

Dressing
2 good teasp. pure Irish honey
1 tablesp. approx. white wine vinegar

Garnish
few leaves of lettuce – green lollo or oakleaf

sprigs of watercress *or* flat parsley chive flowers (optional)

Serves 6

Dissolve the honey in the wine vinegar. Grate both the carrot and apple on the coarse part of the grater, mix together and toss in the sweet and sour dressing. Taste and add a bit more honey or vinegar as required, depending on the sweetness of the apples.

Take 6 white side plates. Arrange a few small lettuce leaves on each plate and divide the salad between the plates. Garnish with watercress or flat parsley and sprinkle with chive flowers if you wish.

v Carrot and Parsnip – Green, White and Gold or Sunshine

T*hese are all popular names for the same much-loved winter vegetable. I infinitely prefer them mashed roughly* *rather than puréed – the rustic rather than the genteel approach!*

8 ozs (225 g/scant 2 cups) Irish
   carrots
12 ozs (340 g/3 cups) parsnips
2 ozs (55 g/½ stick) butter
salt, freshly ground pepper and
   sugar

Garnish
chopped parsley

Serves 4-6

Wash and peel the carrots and
parsnips, removing the core if
necessary. Slice into ¼ inch (5 mm)
slices. Cook the carrots in a little
boiling salted water with a pinch of
sugar until really soft. Cook the
parsnips separately in boiling salted
water.

Strain both, mash them together
with a potato masher, add butter, salt
and lots of freshly ground pepper and
a pinch of sugar if you like. Sprinkle
with chopped parsley and serve,
hence green, white and gold!

v* Carrot and Potato with Cream and Fresh Spices

F*resh spices can add magic to your
cooking. Here they give an altogether
new dimension to carrots and potatoes.*

1 lb (450 g) carrots
2 lbs (900 g) medium potatoes
2½ teasp. cumin seed
3 teasp. coriander seed
1 inch (2.5 cm) piece of
   cinnamon stick
1 teasp. cardamom seed
8 cloves
¼ teasp. black peppercorns
½ oz (15 g) butter
1 large red onion, roughly diced
1 clove of garlic, finely chopped
1 oz (30 g) fresh ginger, peeled
   and grated
¼ teasp. freshly grated nutmeg
½ teasp. turmeric
1 teasp. sugar
½ teasp. salt
1½ lbs (675 g) very ripe tomatoes,
   peeled and chopped
6 fl ozs (175 ml/¾ cup) yoghurt

4-8 fl ozs (120-250 ml/½-1 cup)
   creamy milk
1-2 tablesp. chopped fresh
   coriander

Garnish
sprigs of fresh coriander

Serves 6

Cook the potatoes in boiling salted
water until barely cooked. Scrape or
thinly peel the carrots, cut in ½ inch
(1 cm) thick slices and cook in a little
boiling salted water until almost
tender.

Put the whole spices into a
grinder and grind finely.

Melt the butter in a saucepan and
cook the onion until golden. Add the
garlic, grated ginger, ground spices,
nutmeg, turmeric, sugar and salt.
Cook for 1-2 minutes, then add the
tomato and finally the yoghurt,
stirring well.

Peel the cooked potatoes and cut into ½ inch (1 cm) slices. Add with the carrots to the sauce, add the creamy milk and simmer until the vegetables have finished cooking. Stir in the coriander, taste and correct the seasoning, and serve immediately with a good green salad and some Ballymaloe Tomato Relish.

ᵛ* Potato, Carrot and Cauliflower Curry

Sophie Grigson, the bubbly cook of the many earrings, made this exceptionally delicious vegetable curry when she was guest chef at the Ballymaloe Cookery School recently.

Serves 4

7 ozs (200 g) small new potatoes
   or **waxy salad potatoes**
7 ozs (200 g) cauliflower florets
7 ozs (200 g) carrots, cut at an
   angle
4 green cardamom pods
1 tablesp. (1 American tablesp. +
   1 teasp.) coriander seeds
2 teasp. cumin seeds
2 dried red chillies, deseeded and
   broken into pieces
4 tablesp. (5 American tablesp. +
   1 teasp.) desiccated coconut
1 scant teasp. grated fresh ginger
8 fl ozs (250 ml/1 cup) Greek
   style yoghurt
1½ ozs (45 g/3 American
   tablesp.) butter
2 tablesp. (2½ American tablesp.)
   sunflower oil
1 small onion, grated
salt

Garnish
1 oz (30 g) toasted flaked almonds
1 tablesp. approx. freshly
   chopped coriander

Boil the potatoes in their jackets until just tender. Skin and halve them. Steam or boil the cauliflower until barely cooked. Drain well. Steam or boil the carrots until barely cooked and drain them.

Split the cardamom pods and extract the seeds. Mix with the coriander and cumin seeds. Dry fry in a heavy pan over a high heat until they smell of incense. Tip into a bowl. Dry fry the chilli (which makes it easier to grind) and then add the coconut and fry until pale golden; mix with the spices. Cool, grind to a powder and mix with the ginger and yoghurt.

Melt the butter with the oil and fry the potatoes, cauliflower and carrots briskly until patched with brown. Set aside. Add the onion to the fat and fry until golden brown, then stir in the yoghurt mixture, a tablespoonful at a time. Cook, stirring for 2 minutes, then stir in 2 tablespoons of water, followed by the potatoes and cauliflower. Stir until piping hot, then serve sprinkled with toasted almonds and freshly chopped coriander.

Cauliflower

^{vv} Cauliflower or Broccoli Salad
^{v*} Cauliflower Cheese
Cauliflower Cheese Soup
^{v*} Sicilian Green Cauliflower or Romanesco
with Black Olives

When I was a child, cauliflower was one of the winter vegetables we considered a real treat. We sometimes had Cauliflower Cheese for lunch on Fridays – made from one huge head which miraculously fed all nine of us in one go. What on earth has happened to cauliflower since then? It seems to me that it has suffered, perhaps more than any other vegetable, as a result of intensive production. The curd part now has virtually no flavour – but the leaves have some, so make sure you choose a specimen with as many leaves on as possible.

You need to dress cauliflower up in some way to make it tasty, but there are plenty of possibilities besides cheese sauce. You can put small pieces in batter and deepfry them, or serve it warm with a well flavoured vinaigrette dressing spiced up with a bit of chilli. Cauliflower is really only worth growing if you have plenty of space to spare. Plant some of the old varieties which have more flavour than the bland caulis on sale in the shops – and if you feel like a bit of exoticism, you might also like to try the new purple or green varieties which look splendid in salads.

^{vv} Cauliflower or Broccoli Salad

Cauliflower or broccoli salad is not an obvious choice but it is surprisingly delicious. The secret, as is the case with many salads, is to dip the florets in a good dressing while they are still warm so that they absorb the flavours.

1 head of cauliflower
4 fl ozs (120 ml/½ cup) Billy's French Dressing (see below)

Serves 6

Ideally this should be made with slightly shot heads at the end of the season. Take a head with the leaves on, and trim off the damaged ones. Wash and shred the remaining leaves and stalk, splitting the cauliflower into about 8 pieces so it will cook evenly.

Take a saucepan that fits the cauliflower exactly and boil 1 inch (2.5 cm) of water in it. Add a little salt, put in the shredded leaves, and sit the cauliflower on top, stems down, and cover closely. Control the heat so that it does not boil dry.

Remove from the pot when the stalks are barely tender. Divide into florets. Dip each into French dressing while they are still warm and arrange like a wheel on a round plate. Build up layer upon layer to re-form the cauliflower head. This looks good and tastes delicious on a cold buffet.

Note: Green broccoli (calabrese) or purple or white sprouting broccoli can be cooked this way also and a mixture of all three looks and tastes wonderful.

Billy's French Dressing

6 fl ozs (175 ml/¾ cup) olive oil *or* a mixture of olive and other oils, e.g. sunflower and arachide
2 fl ozs (60 ml/¼ cup) white wine vinegar
1 level teasp.(½ American teasp.) mustard – Dijon *or* English
1 level teasp.(½ American teasp.) salt
a few grinds of pepper
1 large clove of garlic, mashed
sprig of parsley
1 scallion *or* small spring onion
sprig of watercress

Put all the ingredients into a blender and run at medium speed for 1 minute approx., or mix oil and vinegar in a bowl, add mustard, salt, freshly ground pepper and mashed garlic. Chop the parsley, spring onion and watercress finely and add in. Whisk before serving.

ᵛ* Cauliflower Cheese

1 medium-sized cauliflower with green leaves
salt

Mornay Sauce
1 pint (600 ml/2½ cups) milk with a dash of cream
slice of onion
3-4 slices of carrot
6 peppercorns

thyme *or* parsley
roux (see glossary)
salt and freshly ground pepper
4 ozs (110 g/1 cup) grated cheese – Irish Cheddar *or* a mixture of Gruyère, Parmesan and Cheddar
¼ teasp. mustard

1 oz (30 g/¼ cup) grated mature Irish Cheddar cheese for top

Garnish
chopped parsley

Serves 6-8

Remove the outer leaves and wash both the cauliflower and the leaves well. Put not more than 1 inch (2.5 cm) of water in a saucepan just large enough to take the cauliflower; add a little salt. Chop the leaves into small pieces or cut the cauliflower into quarters.

Place the cauliflower on top of the green leaves in the saucepan, cover and simmer until the cauliflower is cooked – 15 minutes approx. Test by piercing the stalk with a knife; there should be just a little resistance. Remove the cauliflower and the leaves to an ovenproof serving dish.

Meanwhile make the Mornay Sauce. Put the cold milk into a saucepan with the onion, carrot, peppercorns and thyme or parsley. Bring to the boil, simmer for 3-4 minutes, remove from the heat and leave to infuse for 10 minutes. Strain out the vegetables, bring the milk back to the boil and thicken with roux to a light coating consistency.

Add 4 ozs (110 g/1 cup) grated cheese and the mustard. Season with salt and freshly ground pepper, taste and correct the seasoning if necessary. Spoon the sauce over the cauliflower and sprinkle with the remainder of the grated cheese. The dish may be prepared ahead to this point.

Put into a hot oven, 230°C/450°F/regulo 8, or under the grill to brown. If the Cauliflower Cheese is allowed to get completely cold, it will take 20-25 minutes to reheat in a moderate oven, 180°C/350°F/regulo 4.

Serve sprinkled with chopped parsley.

Cauliflower Cheese Soup

Follow the recipe for Cauliflower Cheese; but instead of gratinating under the grill, liquidise the lot with any left-over cauliflower cooking water and enough light chicken stock, 1½ pints (900 ml/3¾ cups) approx., to make a nice consistency. Taste and correct the seasoning. Serve with croûtons, cubes of diced Cheddar cheese and parsley.

ᵛ* Sicilian Green Cauliflower or Romanesco with Black Olives

A nna Tasca from Regaleali in Sicily gave me this recipe. We used Romanesco but in Sicily they use the wonderful green cauliflowers which are in season in the autumn.

2 heads of green *or* white cauliflower *or* calabrese – 2 lbs (scant kilo) approx.
1 small onion, minced – 4 ozs (110 g) approx.
4 fl ozs (120 ml/½ cup) extra virgin olive oil
2 ozs (55 g/½ cup) black olives, pitted and sliced
salt and freshly ground black pepper
1 oz (30 g/¼ cup) freshly grated Parmesan *or* Pecorino cheese
8 ozs (225 g) Mozzarella cheese, grated (optional)

Serves 8

Cut the cauliflower or calabrese into 2 inch (5 cm) florets and boil in well salted water until *al dente* – 5 minutes approx. Drain. Meanwhile, sauté the onion in half the olive oil until tender and slightly golden, 3-4 minutes approx. Remove from the heat and add the sliced olives. Set aside.

Preheat the oven to 200°C/ 400°F/regulo 6.

Spread out the cauliflower or calabrese in the dish. Add the onion-olive mixture, the remaining olive oil, salt and freshly ground pepper to taste (remembering that the Parmesan may be salty!). Toss the cauliflower or calabrese mixture with about half of the Parmesan and top with Mozzarella if desired. Sprinkle the remaining Parmesan over the top.

Bake for 20-30 minutes or until the top is nice and golden. Serve warm or at room temperature.

Celery

^v Buttered Celery
^v Celery with Cream and Parsley
Winter Celery Soup with Toasted Hazelnuts
^v Apple, Celery and Walnut Salad
Apple, Celery, Walnut and Chicken Salad

It's sacrilege, I know, but my first reaction as I write the introduction to this section is that I could live my whole life without ever seeing a bit of celery again. But then I think of Winter Celery Soup and crisp Apple, Celery and Walnut Salad and I relent! I know there are a great many people who have no reservations whatsoever about celery. Maybe I bear it some ill will because it is one of the few vegetables with which I have had a singular lack of success in the garden – but that's my ineptitude, and hardly the celery's fault!

Serious gardeners take pride in growing celery well – and non-gardeners can take comfort from the fact that good celery is now available in the shops all year round. Remember that the leaves have a strong, delicious flavour which makes them ideal for soups and salads.

^v Buttered Celery

1 head of celery
1 oz (30 g/¼ stick) butter
salt and freshly ground pepper

Garnish
chopped parsley

Serves 4-6

Pull the stalks off the head of celery. If the outer stalks seem a bit tough, peel the strings off with a swivel top peeler or simply save these tougher stalks for the stock pot. Cut the celery into ½ inch (1 cm) chunks, preferably at an angle.

Bring ¼ pint (150 ml/generous ½ cup) water to the boil, add a little salt and the chopped celery. Cover and cook for 15-20 minutes or until a knife will go through the celery with ease.* Drain, add the butter and season with salt and freshly ground pepper. Serve garnished with chopped parsley.

^v Celery with Cream and Parsley

add to Buttered Celery ingredients:
**4-6 fl ozs (120-175 ml/½-¾ cup)
   cream
roux (see glossary)**

Follow the previous recipe to *
then remove the celery, pour off
most of the water and add the cream,
thicken with a little roux, add the
celery back in and allow to bubble for
a few minutes. Put into a hot serving
dish, sprinkle with parsley and serve.

Winter Celery Soup with Toasted Hazelnuts

**1¼ lbs (560 g/4 cups) celery,
   finely chopped
1½ ozs (45 g) butter
5 ozs (140 g/1 cup) potatoes, cut
   into ¼ inch (5 mm) dice
5 ozs (140 g/1 cup) onion,
   chopped
salt and freshly ground pepper
1½ pints (900 ml/3¾ cups)
   homemade chicken stock
¼-½ pint (150-300 ml/½-1 cup)
   creamy milk**

Garnish
**a few tablesp. whipped cream
2 tablesp. approx. hazelnuts,
   skinned, toasted and chopped
sprigs of chervil *or* flat parsley**

Serves 8-10

Melt the butter in a heavy-
bottomed saucepan. When it
foams, add the potatoes, onion and
celery; toss in the butter until evenly
coated. Season with salt and freshly
ground pepper. Cover with a paper
lid (to keep in the steam) and the
saucepan lid and sweat over a gentle
heat for 10 minutes approx., until the
vegetables are soft but not coloured.

Remove the paper lid, add the
chicken stock and simmer until the
celery is fully cooked, 10-12 minutes
approx. Liquidise the soup, add a
little more stock or creamy milk to
thin to the required consistency.
Taste and correct the seasoning.

Serve the soup piping hot with a
little blob of whipped cream on top.
Sprinkle with the chopped hazelnuts
and sprigs of chervil or flat parsley.

ᵛApple, Celery and Walnut Salad

This is one of the few mixed salad combinations that works really well. The tart mixture of apple and celery makes it an excellent counterbalance to rich meats such as duck or pork, or it may be served as a first course on its own.

½ **head of celery**
8 **ozs (225 g) red dessert apples**
8 **ozs (225 g) green dessert apples**
2 **tablesp. approx. lemon juice**
1 **level teasp. castor sugar**
¼ **pint (150 ml/generous ½ cup)**
    Mayonnaise (see page 30)
2 **ozs (55 g/½ cup) shelled fresh**
    walnuts
1 **crisp lettuce**

Garnish
sprigs of watercress
freshly chopped parsley

Separate the celery, wash it and chop or julienne the stalks into 1½ inch (4 cm) lengths. Put them into a bowl of iced water for 15–30 minutes. Keep aside half a red and half a green apple. Wash and core the remainder, and cut into ½ inch (1 cm) dice.

Make a dressing by mixing the freshly squeezed lemon juice, castor sugar and 1 tablespoon of mayonnaise (reserve a little lemon juice and castor sugar). Toss the diced apple in the dressing and let it stand while you prepare the remainder of the ingredients.

Chop the walnuts roughly. Add the celery and most of the walnuts to the diced apples with the rest of the mayonnaise, and mix thoroughly. Slice the remaining red and green apples and sprinkle them with castor sugar and lemon juice.

Line a serving bowl with the clean crisp lettuce leaves and pile the salad into the centre. Arrange the apple slices around the bowl, alternating red and green. Garnish with sprigs of watercress and scatter some chopped parsley and the remainder of the chopped walnuts over the centre.

Note: To serve as a first course, arrange a few lettuce leaves on a white plate and pile a few tablespoons of salad into the centre. Arrange the slices of the red and green apple around the edge. Garnish with sprigs of watercress, sprinkle with parsley and serve.

Apple, Celery, Walnut and Chicken Salad

As above, but add 2 cooked and sliced chicken breasts to the salad with the celery. Serve as a main course.

Courgettes and Marrows

I would urge everybody who has even the smallest garden to grow courgettes – right there in the middle of your flower bed if necessary, because they are so decorative. Four or five plants will provide more than enough for your family, with extra left over to lavish on friends. By growing them, you have the luxury of being able to pick them, green or golden, at exactly the right stage, when they are less than six inches (15 cm) long and their flavour is sweet and nutty. Any that remain can be left to grow into marrows, which can be made into wonderful soups, stuffed or served simply with a velvety cheese sauce. That may sound dull, but it is completely delicious with a winter roast.

Don't neglect to use the pretty courgette flowers, which for me are the great bonus of growing your own plants. I put them in salads, stuff them and dip them in batter to make crispy fritters, or use them as lovely little containers for sauces to go with cruditées.

* Salad of Prawns and Courgettes

This salad devised by my brother Rory O'Connell both looks and tastes stunning. The courgette (zucchini) flowers are of course edible! This is a perfect recipe for people who grow their own courgettes.

4 small courgettes (zucchini) with flowers (choose shiny, firm courgettes)
24 freshly cooked and shelled prawns
sea salt and freshly ground pepper

Salad of Prawns and Courgettes

Cruditées with Tapenade

Globe Artichokes with Melted Butter

Kinoith Garden Salad

Stuffed Mushrooms

a little extra virgin olive oil
2-3 tablesp. homemade
    Mayonnaise (see page 30)

Garnish
chervil *or* **fennel sprigs**
courgette petals

Serves 4 as a starter

Separate the flowers from the
courgettes. Remove the stamens and
the little thorns from the base of the
flowers.

Plunge the courgettes into boiling
salted water and poach until barely
tender, 4 minutes approx. Remove
from the pot and allow to cool
slightly; they will continue to cook.
While still warm cut them into
¼ inch (5 mm) slices at an angle.

Season immediately with sea salt and
freshly ground pepper, sprinkle with
olive oil and toss gently.

To assemble the salad, arrange
6 courgette slices on each plate and
place a prawn on each slice. Cut the
petals off 4 of the courgette flowers,
1½ inches (4 cm) approx. from the
base – these make pretty edible
containers. Place one in the centre of
each plate, fill with ½ tablespoon of
mayonnaise, using a piping bag if
possible. Garnish the plates with the
courgette petals and sprigs of chervil
or fennel. Serve immediately.

Note: Mussels or shrimps may be
used instead of prawns: allow 6-12
mussels or 12 shrimps per starter
portion. If using lobster allow 2 ozs
(55 g) cooked lobster per portion.

ᵛᵛ* Courgette Flower Salad

T his sounds utterly simple, and indeed
it is – but when the salad is made
with young courgettes, good oil and served
warm it is quite exquisite. The flowers are
a pretty but inessential addition.

6-8 green *or* **golden courgettes** *or*
    a mixture no more than
    6 inches (15 cm) in length
extra virgin olive oil

sea salt
courgette flowers if available

Serves 6-8

Prepare, cook and dress the
courgettes as in the previous recipe.
Serve as soon as possible on a pretty
plate surrounded by the petals of
courgette flowers.

ᵛᵛ* Courgettes with Marjoram

I 'm completely hooked on annual
marjoram. The seed is sometimes
difficult to track down because it can be
called Sweet marjoram or Knotty

marjoram, but if you have any little patch
at all it's worth growing because it
transforms so many dishes into a feast.

1 lb (450 g) green *or* golden
   courgettes *or* a mixture no
   more than 6 inches (15 cm) in
   length
1-2 tablesp. approx. olive oil
1-2 teasp. chopped annual
   marjoram *or* basil

Serves 4

Top and tail the courgettes and cut
them into scant ¼ inch (5 mm) slices.
Heat the oil, toss in the courgettes
and coat in the olive oil. Cook on a
medium heat until just tender – 4-5
minutes approx. Add the marjoram or
basil. Season with salt and freshly
ground pepper. Turn into a hot dish
and serve immediately.

Courgettes are one of the trickier
vegetables to cook. Like mangetout
peas they seem to continue cooking
at an alarming rate after you've taken
them out of the pot, so whip them
out while they are slightly *al dente*.

ᵛ* Courgette and Basil Omelette

T his is one of the flat Mediterranean
   omelettes that are simply divine for a
*summer lunch. Somehow one bite
transports you to the magical world of
Provence!*

10 ozs (285 g) courgettes, no
   more than 6 inches (15 cm) in
   length
5 tablesp. (7 American tablesp.)
   extra virgin olive oil
salt and freshly ground pepper
6 eggs, preferably free-range
1 dessertsp. fresh torn basil leaves
   or annual marjoram
1-2 dessertsp. freshly chopped
   parsley

Garnish
a few basil leaves
6-8 black olives (optional)

Serves 2

Slice the unpeeled courgettes into
very thin rounds. Heat 2 tablespoons
of the oil in a pan, add the courgettes,
season with salt and freshly ground
pepper and cook until *al dente*. Drain.

Whisk the eggs in a bowl, season
with salt and freshly ground pepper,
add the basil and parsley and finally
the courgettes. Heat 2 more
tablespoons of olive oil in a non-stick
frying pan. Pour in the omelette
mixture and cook on a medium heat
stirring gently.

When the omelette is cooked –
set and golden on the bottom but still
juicy on top – place a hot plate over
the top of the pan and with the help
of a tea towel quickly turn it upside
down so the omelette ends up on the
plate golden side upwards. (Easier said
than done!) Drizzle with the
remaining olive oil and scatter basil
leaves and a few black olives if you
like over the top. Serve warm or cold.

* Stuffed Marrow with a Crunchy Top

All manner of stuffings can be devised but ensure that they are tasty and well seasoned, otherwise the end result can be exceedingly dull.

1 marrow, 5½ lb (2.5 kg) approx.

Stuffing
2 tablesp. approx. olive oil
4 ozs (110 g) streaky bacon, diced
4 ozs (110 g/scant 1 cup) onion, chopped
1-2 cloves of garlic, crushed (optional)
4 ozs (110 g) mushrooms, chopped
salt and freshly ground pepper
1 lb (450 g) minced beef
1 tablesp. approx. parsley, 1 dessertsp. thyme and 1 dessertsp. chives, all chopped *or* 2 tablesp. approx. annual marjoram
1 × 14 oz (400 g) tin of tomatoes
salt, freshly ground pepper and sugar

1 pint (600 ml/2½ cups) Mornay Sauce (see page 42)

1 oz (30 g) Buttered Crumbs (see page 65)
1½ ozs (45 g) grated Irish Cheddar cheese

Serves 8-10

First make the stuffing. Heat 1 tablespoon of the oil in a wide saucepan or sauté pan, add the streaky bacon and cook until crisp; remove to a plate. Reduce the heat, add the onion and crushed garlic and sweat for a few minutes; add to the bacon. Increase the heat, add the mushrooms, season with salt and freshly ground pepper, toss for 1-2 minutes and put with the rest.

Add another tablespoon of olive oil to the pan then toss the minced beef on a high heat until it changes colour; next return the onion, bacon and mushrooms. Now for some fresh herbs – marjoram is particularly delicious but a mixture of parsley, chives and thyme or even some rosemary would be very good also. Then add the tomatoes, season with salt, freshly ground pepper and a good pinch of sugar, particularly if you are using tinned tomatoes. Increase the heat and cook until the mixture is thick and concentrated but still juicy.

Meanwhile make the Mornay Sauce.

Preheat the oven to 180°C/ 350°F/regulo 4. Split the marrow in half lengthwise and scoop out the seeds from one half. Cover the other half and save for another recipe – perhaps marrow in cheese sauce (one of my favourite things in the whole world!).

When the stuffing has reduced, taste and correct the seasoning: it should be intense and lively. Season the cavity of the marrow with salt and freshly ground pepper and a sprig or two of marjoram if you have it. Fill with stuffing.

Coat with thick, well seasoned Mornay Sauce and sprinkle the top generously with a mixture of grated cheese and Buttered Crumbs. Bake in the preheated oven for 1 hour approx. – the marrow should be very tender. It is cooked when a knife will pierce it without any resistance.

Serve with garlic butter and a good green salad.

^v Individual Portions of Stuffed Marrow

Cut a circular piece of marrow 1½ inches (4 cm) thick approx. Scoop out the centre, fill with Tomato Fondue (see page 15), Piperonata or any filling of your choice. Coat with Mornay Sauce (see page 42), sprinkle with a mixture of Buttered Crumbs and grated cheese. Bake in a moderate oven, 180°C/350°F/regulo 4, for 15-20 minutes approx. Serve with garlic butter.

^v Spaghetti Marrow

Cook the whole spaghetti marrow in boiling salted water until tender, anything from 15-45 minutes depending on the size. Split in half (it will look like spaghetti inside) and serve with garlic butter or tomato sauce or – better still – both.

Spaghetti marrow with garlic butter is particularly good as an accompaniment to Shepherd's Pie.

Cucumber

v* Lebanese Cold Cucumber Soup
v* Cucumber Ring with Tomato and Coriander
v Greek Salad
v Cucumber Neapolitana
v Tzatziki

Even though cucumbers are in the shops now all year round, the crisp and juicy Irish ones are worth waiting for after the limp and bitter plastic-clad imported specimens to which we are subjected for most of the winter. Unless you are a wizard gardener, however, cucumbers are quite a challenge to grow. For good results you will need a greenhouse, and they require a fair amount of attention and expertise.

v* Lebanese Cold Cucumber Soup

This cooling summer soup can be adapted to make a cucumber ring to which can be added a variety of tasty fillings.

1 large cucumber
8 fl ozs (250 ml/1 cup) light
  cream
4 fl ozs (120 ml/½ cup) natural
  yoghurt
2 tablesp. (2½ American tablesp.)
  tarragon vinegar
½ or 1 clove of garlic, crushed
1 tablesp. approx. finely chopped
  gherkins
2 tablesp. approx. finely chopped
  mint
salt and freshly ground pepper

Garnish
sprigs of mint

Serves 8-10

Grate the cucumber on the coarsest part of the grater. Stir in all the other ingredients. Season well. Serve chilled in small bowls, garnished with a sprig of mint.

v* Cucumber Ring with Tomato and Coriander

1 pint (600 ml/2½ cups) Lebanese
  Cold Cucumber Soup (see
  page 53)
¼ oz (8 g/2 rounded teasp.)
  gelatine
2 tablesp. (2½ American tablesp.)
  water

Tomato and Coriander Sauce
6 fl ozs (175 ml/¾ cup) natural
  yoghurt
3 fl ozs (85 ml) Fresh Tomato
  Juice (see opposite)
2 tablesp. approx. cream
1 tablesp. approx. fresh coriander
salt, freshly ground pepper and
  sugar

Garnish
4 very ripe Irish tomatoes tossed
  in French Dressing (see page
  42) with salt, pepper, sugar
  and freshly chopped mint
½ Irish cucumber approx., peeled
  and cut into batons, seasoned
  with salt, pepper, sugar and
  finely chopped fennel
6 tiny leaves of lettuce
6 tiny spring onions
6 sprigs of watercress

6 small ring moulds *or* 1 large
  ring mould

Serves 6

Sprinkle the gelatine over the
water in a bowl, allow to sponge,
then dissolve in a saucepan of
simmering water until all the granules
are melted. Mix some of the cold
soup with the gelatine and then stir
into the remainder of the mixture,
stirring very well. Pour into 1 large or
6 small oiled ring moulds. Chill until
set.

Meanwhile make the sauce. Mix
the yoghurt with the well seasoned
fresh tomato juice, add the cream and
coriander, season with salt, pepper
and sugar, taste and adjust seasoning if
necessary.

To assemble: Cut the tomatoes
into 4 or 6 pieces, toss in a little
French Dressing and season with salt,
pepper, sugar and some fresh mint.
Prepare the cucumber batons. Cut
the cucumber into 2-inch (5 cm) ×
¼ inch (5 mm) batons, season with
salt, freshly ground pepper and sugar
and a little fennel. Turn the
cucumber ring or rings onto white
plates, pour a little sauce into the
centre and around the sides, arrange a
lettuce leaf, piece of tomato and a
few cucumber batons in the centre.
Garnish with a spring onion and
some fresh watercress and serve.

Note: A large ring mould will take
2 pints (1200 ml) cold cucumber
soup.

VV FRESH TOMATO JUICE

This is worth making only when you have very well flavoured vine-ripened tomatoes.

1 lb (450 g/2½ cups roughly filled) very ripe Irish tomatoes, peeled and halved
1 spring onion with a little green leaf *or* 1 slice of onion 2 inch (5 cm) diameter and ¼ inch (5 mm) thick
3 basil *or* mint leaves
2 teasp. white wine vinegar

1 tablesp. olive oil
4 fl ozs (120 ml/½ cup) cold water
1 level teasp. salt
1 level teasp. sugar
a few grinds of black pepper

Liquidise the ingredients together, then strain. Best when freshly made and better kept for not more than 12 hours. Boil up left-overs for a purée instead.

^v Greek Salad

This salad is served everywhere in Greece and is delicious when made with best and freshest ingredients. We use our local Knockalara ewe's milk cheese instead of Feta which is seldom in the condition that the Greeks intended by the time it reaches us!

⅓-½ crisp Irish cucumber
6 very ripe Irish tomatoes
6 scallions
12 Kalamati olives
2 tablesp. approx. chopped annual marjoram
extra virgin olive oil
freshly squeezed lemon juice
salt, freshly cracked pepper and sugar
2-3 ozs (55-85 g) crumbled Knockalara ewe's milk cheese★ *or* fresh Feta cheese

sprigs of flat parsley

Serves 6

Core the tomatoes and cut into wedges. Halve the cucumber and cut into chunks, and chop the green and white parts of the scallions. Mix the tomatoes, cucumber, scallions, olives and marjoram in a bowl, and sprinkle with olive oil and lemon juice. Season with salt, freshly cracked pepper and sugar and toss well. Sprinkle with roughly crumbled cheese and sprigs of flat parsley and serve at once.

Note: Slices of red pepper may be included.

★Knockalara cheese, Cappoquin, Co. Waterford, Phone 024-96326.

^V Cucumber Neapolitana

T *his is a very versatile vegetable dish which can be made ahead of time and reheats well. It is also delicious as a stuffing for tomatoes and is particularly good with lamb.*

1 Irish cucumber
½ oz (15 g/⅛ stick) butter
1 medium onion – 4 ozs (110 g) approx., sliced
4 very ripe Irish tomatoes
salt and freshly ground pepper
2½ fl ozs (63 ml/generous ¼ cup) cream
1 dessertsp. approx. freshly chopped mint
roux (optional – see glossary)

Serves 6 approx.

Melt the butter in a heavy-bottomed saucepan and when it foams add the onion. Cover and sweat for 5 minutes approx. until soft but not coloured.

Meanwhile, peel the cucumber and cut into ½ inch (1 cm) cubes; add to the onion, toss well and continue to cook while you scald the tomatoes with water for 10 seconds. Peel the tomatoes and slice into the casserole, season with salt, freshly ground pepper and a pinch of sugar.

Cover the casserole and cook for a few minutes until the cucumbers are tender and the tomatoes have softened. Add the cream and bring back to the boil. Add the freshly chopped mint. If the liquid is very thin, thicken it by carefully whisking in a little roux. Cucumber Neapolitana keeps for several days and can be reheated.

^V Tzatziki

T *his Greek speciality is a delicious cucumber and yoghurt mixture and can be served as an accompanying salad or as a sauce to serve with grilled fish or meat. Greek yoghurt is often made with sheep's milk and is wonderfully thick and creamy.*

1 crisp Irish cucumber, peeled and finely diced
1-2 cloves of garlic, crushed
dash of wine vinegar *or* lemon juice
1 heaped tablesp. freshly chopped mint

¾ pint (450 ml) Greek yoghurt or best quality natural yoghurt
4 tablesp. cream
chopped fresh mint to taste
salt and freshly ground pepper

Put the cucumber dice into a sieve, sprinkle with salt and allow to drain for about 30 minutes. Dry the cucumber on kitchen paper, put into a bowl and mix with the garlic, the dash of wine vinegar or lemon juice and the yoghurt and cream. Stir in the mint and taste; it may need a little salt and freshly ground pepper, or even a pinch of sugar.

Globe Artichokes

^v Globe Artichokes with Melted Butter
^{vv} Globe Artichokes with Vinaigrette Dressing
^v Globe Artichokes with Hollandaise Sauce

Even if you don't have a vegetable garden at all, globe artichokes are worth considering because these giant, thistle-like plants can look spectacular as a back-drop to flower beds. Their fluffy purple flower heads can be used to stunning effect in dried flower arrangements, but of course artichokes are also marvellous to eat. Rather than sow new seed, try to beg for a shoot from a friend with long-established globe artichokes, as the old varieties (such as Purple Globe) have better flavour.

Eating an artichoke can be quite daunting unless you have seen somebody doing it first. But it's simple, really – and when you've nibbled the ends off all the leaves, and eventually get to the heart of the matter, it will have been worth all the effort. As whole globe artichokes are eaten with the fingers, don't forget to provide little finger-bowls for your guests.

^v Globe Artichokes with Melted Butter

Whole Globe artichokes are quite fiddly to eat. First you pull off each leaf separately and dip it in the sauce. Eventually you are rewarded for your patience when you come to the heart! Don't forget to scrape off the tickly 'choke'; then cut the heart into manageable pieces, and sprinkle with a little sea salt before you dip it into the remainder of your sauce. Simply Delicious!

6 globe artichokes
2 pints (1.1 L/5 cups) water
2 teasp. salt

2 tablesp. approx. white wine vinegar

Melted Butter
6 ozs (170 g/1½ sticks) butter
freshly squeezed juice of ¼ lemon approx.

Serves 6

Some restaurants do very complicated preparation but I merely trim the base just before cooking so that the artichokes will sit steadily on the plate, rub the cut end with lemon juice or vinegar to prevent it from discolouring.

Have a large saucepan of boiling water ready, add 2 teaspoons salt and 2 tablespoons of vinegar to every 2 pints of water, pop in the artichokes and bring the water back to the boil. Simmer steadily for 25 minutes approx. After about 20 minutes you could try testing to see if they are done. I do this by tugging off one of the larger leaves at the base. It should come away easily; if it doesn't, continue to cook for another 5-10 minutes. Remove and drain upside down on a plate.

While they are cooking, simply melt the butter and add lemon juice to taste.

To serve: Put each warm artichoke on to a hot serving plate and serve the sauce or melted butter in a little bowl beside it. Artichokes are eaten with the fingers, so you might like to provide a finger-bowl. A spare plate to collect all the nibbled leaves will also be useful.

ᵛᵛ Globe Artichokes with Vinaigrette Dressing

Ingredients as for previous recipe excluding melted butter section.

Vinaigrette Dressing
2 fl ozs (60 ml/¼ cup) wine vinegar
6 fl ozs (175 ml/¾ cup) olive oil *or* a mixture of olive and other oils, e.g. sunflower and arachide
1 level teasp. (½ American teasp.) mustard, Dijon *or* English
1 large clove of garlic, mashed
1 scallion *or* small spring onion, sprig of parsley and sprig of watercress, all finely chopped

1 level teasp. (½ American teasp.) salt
a few grinds of pepper

Put all the ingredients into a blender and run at medium speed for 1 minute approx., or mix oil and vinegar in a bowl, add the mustard, salt, freshly ground pepper and mashed garlic, chopped parsley, spring onion and watercress. Whisk before serving.

Cook the artichokes as above. Serve little bowls of Vinaigrette Dressing with the warm artichokes.

ᵛ Globe Artichokes with Hollandaise Sauce

Ingredients as for Globe Artichokes with Melted Butter, excluding melted butter section.

Hollandaise Sauce – see page 2

Cook the artichokes as above. Make the Hollandaise Sauce and serve it in little bowls with the warm artichokes.

Jerusalem Artichokes

Jerusalem Artichoke Soup with Crispy Croûtons
ᵛᵛ Warm Salad of Jerusalem Artichokes with
Hazelnut Oil Dressing
Scallops with Jerusalem Artichokes
and Beurre Blanc Sauce

I am delighted that this forgotten vegetable is now making a comeback. For anyone who has the space, Jerusalem artichokes are an absolute doddle to grow. They are a real gem from the gardener's point of view because the foliage grows into a hedge and provides shelter and cover for both compost heaps and pheasants!

The main disadvantage of shop-bought artichokes (when you can find them) is that they may have been out of the ground for days, or even weeks, and as a result the little knobbly brutes are extraordinarily hard to peel. The great thing about growing your own is that if you wash them the minute they are dug you can often get away without peeling them at all.

Jerusalem Artichoke Soup with Crispy Croûtons

2½ lbs (1.15 kg) artichokes,
   peeled and chopped
2 ozs (55 g/½ stick) butter
1¼ lbs (560 g/3¾ cups) potatoes,
   peeled and chopped
salt and freshly ground pepper
2 pints (1.1 L/5 cups) light
   chicken stock
1 pint (600 ml/2½ cups) approx.
   creamy milk

Garnish
freshly chopped parsley
crisp, golden croûtons

Melt the butter in a heavy-bottomed saucepan, add the onions, potatoes and artichokes. Season with salt and freshly ground pepper, cover and sweat gently for 10 minutes approx. Add the stock and cook until the vegetables are soft. Liquidise and return to the heat. Thin to the required flavour and consistency with creamy milk, and adjust the seasoning.

Serve in soup bowls or in a soup tureen, garnished with chopped parsley and crisp, golden croûtons.

Serves 8-10

Jerusalem Artichoke Soup with Crispy Bacon Croûtons

Cut 2 ozs (55 g) streaky bacon into lardons, fry in a little oil until crisp and golden. Drain on kitchen paper, mix with the croûtons and add to the soup just before serving.

ᵛᵛ Warm Salad of Jerusalem Artichokes with Hazelnut Oil Dressing

White turnips or kohlrabi are also delicious cooked and served in exactly the same way as this.

12 ozs (340 g) Jerusalem artichokes, very carefully peeled to a smooth shape
scrap of butter
salt and freshly ground pepper

Hazelnut Oil Dressing
1½ tablesp. (2 American tablesp.) hazelnut oil
1½ tablesp. (2 American tablesp.) sunflower oil
1½ tablesp. (2 American tablesp.) white wine vinegar
a spot of Dijon mustard
salt, freshly ground pepper and sugar to taste

Garnish
½ oz (15 g) hazelnuts, chopped
a few leaves of oakleaf lettuce
sprigs of chervil

Serves 4

Slice the artichokes ⅓ inch (7 mm) thick approx. Bring 4 fl ozs (120 ml) water and the butter to the boil in a heavy saucepan and add the sliced artichokes. Season with salt and freshly ground pepper. Put a lid on the saucepan and simmer gently until the artichokes are completely cooked. The maddening thing about artichokes is that they cook unevenly so it will be necessary to test them with a skewer at regular intervals – they usually take at least 15 minutes.

While the artichokes are cooking, prepare the Hazelnut Dressing by mixing all the ingredients together.

When the artichokes are cooked, carefully remove from the saucepan, making sure not to break them up. Place on a flat dish in a single layer. Spoon over most of the Hazelnut Dressing and toss while still warm.

To assemble the salad: Divide the sliced artichokes between 4 plates. Put a little circle of lettuce around the vegetables and sprinkle the remaining dressing over the lettuce. Garnish with the sliced hazelnuts and chervil sprigs. This salad is best when the artichokes are served while still warm.

Scallops with Jerusalem Artichokes and Beurre Blanc Sauce

Jerusalem artichokes have a wonderful affinity with shellfish, particularly scallops and mussels. This is an exquisite dish worth the little extra effort.

8 scallops
2-4 Jerusalem artichokes
depending on size
1 oz (30 g/¼ stick) butter
a squeeze of fresh lemon juice
salt and freshly ground pepper
Beurre Blanc Sauce (see below)

Garnish
chervil *or* fennel sprigs

Serves 2 as a main course

First prepare the scallops. Wash and slice the nuggets in half horizontally, keeping the corals whole. Keep chilled.

Next make the Beurre Blanc Sauce and keep warm.

Wash and peel the artichokes and cut into ½ inch (1 cm) rounds. Put them into a casserole with the butter and a squeeze of lemon juice (to prevent discoloration). Season with salt and freshly ground pepper, cover and cook gently until just tender.

To assemble the dish: Cook the seasoned scallops on a non-stick pan until golden on each side. Put 2-3 tablespoons (2½-4 American tablespoons) of Beurre Blanc Sauce on to each hot plate. Put 4 artichoke rounds on top of the sauce on each plate. Divide the cooked scallops between the 2 plates, placing half of them on top of the 4 artichoke rounds. Put the coral in the centre, garnish with chervil or fennel and serve immediately.

BEURRE BLANC SAUCE
3 tablesp. (4 American tablesp.)
white wine
3 tablesp. (4 American tablesp.)
white wine vinegar
1 tablesp. approx. finely chopped
shallots
1 generous tablesp. (1½ American
tablesp.) cream
6 ozs (170 g/1½ sticks) cold
unsalted butter, cut into cubes
salt
pinch of ground white pepper
freshly squeezed lemon juice

Put the wine, wine vinegar, shallots and pepper into a heavy-bottomed stainless steel saucepan and reduce to ½ tablespoon approx. Add the cream and boil again until it thickens. Whisk in the cold butter in little pieces, keeping the sauce just warm enough to absorb the butter. Strain out the shallots, season with salt, white pepper and lemon juice and keep warm in a bowl over hot but not simmering water. Add a little hot water if the sauce becomes too think.

Leeks

Winter Leek and Potato Soup
vv Leek Vinaigrette
vv Leek Vinaigrette Terrine with Beetroot Sauce
v Leeks with Yellow Peppers and Marjoram
v Leek and Yellow Pepper Tartlet
Cod with Leeks and Buttered Crumbs

I began to see exciting new possibilities for leeks when I first ate them, tender and pencil-thin, fresh from Raymond Blanc's garden at Le Manoir aux Quat' Saisons outside Oxford. This is another vegetable which can be enjoyed at several stages of its development. It isn't necessary to let leeks grow into prize specimens. Indeed, many of the big fat leeks in the shops have a hard central core which means that they are past their best and already going to seed. The other infuriating thing about shop leeks is that the green tops, so delicious in soups, have often been cut off.

Leeks are slightly more fiddly to plant than some other vegetables, but can be worth it to see you through the winter as they are often quite expensive to buy. There are now some exciting purple varieties which you might like to try.

Winter Leek and Potato Soup

12 ozs (340 g) white parts of the leeks, sliced (save the green tops for another soup or vegetable stock)
2 ozs (55 g/½ stick) butter
1 lb (450 g) potatoes, peeled and cut into ¼ inch (5 mm) dice
4 ozs (110 g) onions, peeled and cut into ¼ inch (5 mm) dice
salt and freshly ground pepper
1½ pints (900 ml/3¾ cups) light homemade chicken stock

2 fl ozs (50 ml) cream
5 fl ozs (150 ml) milk

Garnish
finely chopped chives

Serves 6-8

Melt the butter in a heavy saucepan. When it foams, add the potatoes, onion and leeks and turn them in the butter until well coated. Sprinkle with salt and freshly ground pepper. Cover with a paper lid (to keep in the steam) and the saucepan lid, and sweat on a gentle heat for 10 minutes, or until the vegetables are soft but not coloured. Discard the paper lid. Add the stock; boil until the vegetables are just cooked. Do not overcook or the vegetables will lose their flavour. Liquidise until smooth and silky, taste and adjust the seasoning. Add cream or creamy milk to taste.

Garnish with a blob of cream and some freshly chopped chives.

ᵛᵛ Leek Vinaigrette

T*he secret of this recipe is to toss the leeks in vinaigrette while they are still warm.*

8 medium-sized leeks
3-4 tablesp. (4-5 American
tablesp.) Billy's French
Dressing (see page 42)

Serves 8

Trim the leeks down to the pale end (save the trimmings for the stock pot). Clean thoroughly under running water and poach gently in a little boiling salted water until just tender.

Alternatively cut the leeks into ½ inch (1 cm) rounds at an angle, and poach in a covered saucepan in a very little boiling salted water.

Remove the leeks from the water with a perforated spoon and allow to cool for a few minutes. Coat with French dressing while still warm and leave to marinate. The leeks may be served as a first course, or an accompanying salad, or as part of a selection of salads.

ᵛᵛ Leek Vinaigrette Terrine with Beetroot Sauce

T rim all the leeks to the same size and cook them whole, following the Leek Vinaigrette recipe above. When the warm leeks have been tossed in French dressing, arrange them in layers in a lined terrine, cover and gently press with a board and light weight.

Next day, turn out and cut into thick slices with the utmost care. Serve with lots of crusty white bread and a Beetroot Sauce made from puréed Pickled Beetroot and Onion Salad (see page 18), from which the onion has been omitted.

ᵛ Leeks with Yellow Peppers and Marjoram

T his mixture is also irresistible served in crispy shortcrust tartlets or filo triangles.

6 young leeks, 1 inch (2.5 cm) in diameter approx.
3 yellow peppers
½ oz (15 g/⅛ stick) butter
1 tablesp. approx. extra virgin olive oil
scrap of extra butter
1 tablesp. approx. water
sea salt and freshly ground pepper
1-2 tablesp. approx. fresh annual marjoram *or* a mixture of parsley, basil and marjoram, chopped

Wash and slice the leeks in ¼ inch (5 mm) rounds. Quarter the peppers and cut into ¼ inch (5 mm) thick slices on the bias. Melt the butter and olive oil together in a heavy-bottomed saucepan or casserole, toss in the leeks and add a very little butter and water. Season with salt and freshly ground pepper. Cover and sweat on a gentle heat for 8 minutes approx. or until tender. Add the peppers, toss and add a drop more water if necessary, add half the herbs, cover and continue to cook until the peppers are soft. Taste, add the remainder of the herbs, correct the seasoning and serve.

Serves 6

ᵛ Leek and Yellow Pepper Tartlet

F ill fully baked shortcrust pastry tartlet tins with about 2 tablespoons of the hot leek and yellow pepper mixture above and serve immediately.

Alternatively, prebake tartlet shells, whisk 6 fl ozs (175 ml/¾ cup) cream with 2 egg yolks, combine with the leek and pepper mixture, season and fill into the tartlets. Bake in a moderate oven, 180°C/ 350°F/regulo 4, for 15 minutes approx.

Cod with Leeks and Buttered Crumbs

F resh fish with a crunchy topping in a creamy sauce is always tempting. The gentle flavour of buttered leeks is particularly good with fish.

1 lb 14 ozs (850 kg) hake, cod, ling, haddock, grey sea mullet *or* pollock
salt and freshly ground pepper

Chicken Breasts with Mushrooms and Rosemary

Onion Bhajis with Tomato and Chilli Sauce

Roast Garlic

Pissaladière

Green Pea Soup with Fresh Mint Cream

Mornay Sauce – see page 42

Buttered Crumbs
½ oz (15 g/⅛ stick) butter
1 oz (30 g/½ cup) soft white
    breadcrumbs

1 oz (30 g/¼ stick) butter
1 lb (450 g) leeks, finely sliced
salt and freshly ground pepper
1 tablesp. approx. chopped
    parsley
1½ ozs (45 g) Irish Cheddar
    cheese, grated
1¾ lbs (800 g) Duchesse potato
    (optional)

Serves 6-12, depending on whether it is a main course or a starter

First make the Mornay Sauce.

Next make the Buttered Crumbs. Melt the butter in a pan and stir in the breadcrumbs. Remove from the heat immediately and allow to cool.

Melt the butter in a casserole and toss in the leeks, season with salt and freshly ground pepper, cover and sweat on a gentle heat for 8-10 minutes approx. Add the chopped parsley and keep aside.

Skin the fish and cut into portions: 5 ozs (140 g) for a main course, 2½ ozs (70 g) for a starter. Season with salt and freshly ground pepper. Cover the base of a lightly buttered ovenproof dish with a layer of buttered leeks, lay the pieces of fish on top and coat with the Mornay Sauce.

Mix the grated cheese with the buttered crumbs and sprinkle over the top. Pipe a ruff of fluffy Duchesse potato around the edge if you want to have a whole meal in one dish.

Cook in a moderate oven, 180°C/350°F/regulo 4, for 25-30 minutes or until the fish is cooked through and the top is golden brown and crispy. If necessary flash under the grill for a minute or two before you serve, to brown the edges of the potato.

Note: Cod with Leeks and Buttered Crumbs may be served in individual dishes. Scallop shells are very attractive, completely ovenproof and may be used over and over again.

Lettuce and Salad Leaves

vv **Kinoith Garden Salad with Timmy's Dressing**
vv **Winter Garden Salad with Herbed Vinaigrette Dressing**
* **A Warm Salad of Lamb's Kidneys with
Oyster Mushrooms and Pink Peppercorns**
vv **Wilted Greens**
* **Yuk Sum**
*v** **Radis au Beurre**

Visitors to our ornamental kitchen garden have been charmed all summer long by the array of different lettuces with their green and copper-tinged leaves – crisp and soft, frilly and frizzy. Up to very recently, lettuce was lettuce as far as we were all concerned – and that lettuce was the soft butterhead. Now many shops sell three or four different kinds – but the rarer ones can be shockingly expensive and often in lamentable condition. It comes as a surprise to many people to hear that these exotic types are incredibly easy to grow, and many of the older varieties are actually more resistant to disease. Splash out on a few packets of interesting lettuce and salad leaf seeds (see page xvi for stockists). The Mediterranean mixture variously called *mesculun*, *saladisi* or just Mixed Salad Leaves is tremendously worthwhile – even grown on a seed tray on your windowsill – because as you cut it, it grows again. Even in a tiny garden you can squeeze in a few rows of lettuces, popping the plants into spaces in your flower beds if need be.

vv Kinoith Garden Salad with Timmy's Dressing

Visitors to this country complain over and over again that it is virtually impossible to get a green salad in a restaurant. It does in fact appear on menus regularly but when it is served it often includes tomato, cucumber, pepper and sometimes even raw onion rings – not the mixture of lettuce and salad leaves that people had hoped for. Keep it simple. Be sure to wash and dry the leaves well, tear them in bite-sized pieces, toss in well seasoned dressing made with really good oil and vinegar and include a few edible flowers if the fancy takes you.

This is a rather elaborate version which we make in summer from what is in season in the garden. My husband Timmy's dressing makes it extra special!

a selection of fresh lettuces, salad leaves and edible flowers might include some or all of the following depending on what is available: butterhead, oakleaf, iceberg, saladisi, lollo rosso, frisée, mizuna, purslane, red orach, rocket (*Arugula*), edible chrysanthemum leaves, wild sorrel leaves *or* buckler leaf sorrel, golden marjoram, salad burnet, borage,

courgette *or* squash blossoms, sage flowers, nasturtium flowers and tiny leaves, marigold petals (*Calendula*), chive *or* wild garlic flowers
herb leaves, e.g. lemon balm, mint, flat parsley
tiny sprigs of tarragon *or* dill *or* annual marjoram

TIMMY'S DRESSING
4 tablesp. (5 American tablesp. + 1 teasp.) extra virgin olive oil
1 tablesp. approx. white wine vinegar
1 teasp. pure Irish honey
1 teasp. grainy mustard (we use Lakeshore with honey)
1 clove of garlic, crushed
salt and freshly ground pepper

Whisk all the ingredients together, store in a screw-top jar and shake again to re-emulsify if not serving immediately.

^{vv} Winter Garden Salad with Herbed Vinaigrette Dressing

For this salad, use a selection of winter lettuces and salad leaves, e.g. butterhead, iceberg, frisée, radicchio, endive, chicory and sorrel. Tips of purple sprouting broccoli are also delicious and if you feel like something more robust, use some finely shredded Savoy cabbage and maybe a few shreds of red cabbage also.

Herbed Vinaigrette Dressing
6 fl ozs (175 ml/¾ cup) extra virgin olive oil
4 tablesp. (80 ml) cider vinegar
1 teasp. Irish honey
1 clove garlic, crushed
2 tablesp. approx. freshly chopped mixed herbs – parsley, chives, mint, watercress, thyme
salt and freshly ground pepper

First make the dressing. Put all the dressing ingredients into a screw-top jar adding salt and freshly ground pepper to taste. Shake well to emulsify before use, otherwise whizz all the ingredients together in a food processor or liquidiser for a few seconds. As a variation you could use 4 tablespoons of fresh lemon juice or wine vinegar instead of cider vinegar.

Wash and dry the lettuces and salad leaves and tear into bite-sized pieces. Put them into a deep salad bowl, add the sliced cabbage and toss it all together.

Just before serving, add a little dressing and toss until the leaves glisten.

Note: This makes a fairly large quantity of dressing but it will keep for several days in the fridge. Shake well to re-emulsify before use.

* A Warm Salad of Lamb's Kidneys with Oyster Mushrooms and Pink Peppercorns

a selection of lettuce leaves –
   butterhead, iceberg,
   radicchio, Chinese leaves,
   lamb's lettuce *or* rocket
2-3 lamb's kidneys
4 ozs (110 g) oyster mushrooms
a little olive oil
1 tablesp. approx. annual
   marjoram, freshly chopped
   (optional)

Vinaigrette Dressing
1 tablesp. (1 American tablesp. +
   1 teasp.) arachide *or*
   sunflower oil
2 tablesp. extra virgin olive oil
1 tablesp. (1 American tablesp. +
   1 teasp.) wine vinegar
¼ teasp. Dijon mustard
salt and freshly ground pepper

Garnish
30 pink peppercorns (optional)

Serves 6

Remove the skin and fatty membrane from the centre of the kidneys, and cut the flesh into small cubes, ½ inch (1 cm) approx. Trim the stalks from the mushrooms and slice lengthwise. Wash the lettuces and dry carefully. Heat the olive oil in a frying pan until it smokes, toss in the mushrooms, season and fry quickly for 3-4 minutes approx., add the marjoram and remove to a hot plate.

Add the kidneys to the pan and fry quickly for 2 minutes approx. While the kidneys are cooking, toss the lettuce in a little of the dressing and divide between the plates. Spoon the hot kidneys and the mushrooms over the salad immediately they are cooked; if liked, scatter salad with pink peppercorns; serve immediately.

Note: Use chive flowers or marigold petals as a garnish if you don't have pink peppercorns.

ᵛᵛ Wilted Greens

This is a perfectly delicious and extremely fashionable new way of eating the tender and enormously nutritious young leaves of vegetables. Try the wilted greens with salmon, coarse terrines, juicy steaks or chops.

mixture of young vegetable leaves – tiny beetroot leaves, Swiss chard, spinach, carrot tops, sorrel, rocket – allow 1 fistful per person approx.
1-2 tablesp. approx. extra virgin olive oil
¼-½ red chilli, chopped and deseeded
clove of garlic, chopped
salt and freshly ground pepper

Serves 4

Heat the oil in a pan and add the chopped garlic and chilli. Add in the leaves, toss well for a few seconds until they just begin to wilt, season with salt and freshly ground pepper. Taste, and serve immediately.

* Yuk Sum

Don't let the name put you off! When my brother Rory and I came across this extraordinary-sounding dish on a menu in a Chinese restaurant in Birmingham we couldn't resist the temptation. It turned out to be a delicious pork dish, served on lettuce leaves which are used to make little parcels as you eat it. This is my interpretation, which although not authentic Cantonese, wins lots of compliments.

8 ozs (225 g) minced streaky pork
2 tablesp. approx. olive oil
1 teasp. freshly grated ginger
2 tablesp. approx. spring onion
2 ozs (55 g) mushrooms, chopped
1 oz (30 g) celery, finely chopped
salt and freshly ground pepper
1 tablesp. approx. oyster sauce
iceberg lettuce leaves

Garnish
⅓ cucumber approx., cut into ¼ inch (5 mm) thick julienne strips
8 spring onion 'sweeping brushes'

Serves 4

Heat a wok until very hot, add the olive oil, grated ginger and spring onion, and toss for a second or two. Next add the pork, cook on a high heat until almost done, then push the pork up to the side of the wok. Add the chopped mushrooms and toss until cooked. Add the celery and mix with the mushrooms and pork. Season with salt and freshly ground pepper, and add the oyster sauce. Toss for 1-2 minutes more. Taste and correct the seasoning.

Put some crisp iceberg lettuce on to a plate, and spoon 1-2 tablespoons of the pork mixture into the centre of each. Garnish the plate with julienne strips of cucumber and a couple of spring onion 'sweeping brushes'. Eat immediately by wrapping the pork, cucumber and spring onion in the lettuce to make a parcel.

^{v*} Radis au Beurre

The French know one of the most delicious ways to eat radishes. First you put a dab of butter on a radish, then you dip it into some sea salt, then you eat it with some crusty white bread. You could be arrested for suggesting such a thing in these crazy low-fat low-salt days, but the French have been eating radishes like this for generations and are doing well, thank you very much!

1 bunch of very fresh radishes
2-3 unsalted butter pats
sea salt
crusty white bread

Serves 1

Wash the radishes gently and remove the root end. Trim the leaves 1 inch (2.5 cm) approx. above the top. Serve on a plate with unsalted butter, crystals of sea salt and some crusty white French bread.

Mixed Vegetable Dishes

A Plate of Garden Salads
v *Warm Vegetable Salad with Summer Herbs*
Cruditées with Tapenade
*vv** *Tian of Mediterranean Vegetables Baked with
Olive Oil and Herbs*
*v** *Rustic Mediterranean Sandwich*
vv *Vegetable Stew with Fresh Spices and
Banana and Yoghurt Raita*
vv *Indian Spiced Vegetable Pakoras with Mango Relish*
v *Courgette and Basil Lasagne*

I hope that all of this book will have a special appeal for vegetarians, and those who cook for them. For this section I have chosen a variety of dishes, many of which are substantial enough to provide a nutritious and exciting main course. They are only the tip of the iceberg, of course. There are infinite variations on these themes, using different combinations of vegetables with pulses, grains and pasta – spiced with imagination!

* A Plate of Garden Salads

We frequently serve a selection of *vegetable salads on a plate as a starter or main course.*

A summer selection might include:
**Red and Yellow Tomato Salad
with Mint *or* Basil
(see page 121)**
cucumber salad

courgette salad
a few radishes
**Mushroom and Caramelised
Onion Salad (see page 82)**
Green Salad (see page 72)
egg mayonnaise (optional)
**Potato and Scallion Salad
(see page 107)**

A winter selection might include:
Potato and Scallion Salad
(see page 107)
Pickled Beetroot and Onion
Salad (see page 18)
cucumber salad
Winter Garden Salad
(see page 67)

Carrot and Apple Salad
(see page 38)
Onions or Leeks Monégasque
(see page 90)
egg mayonnaise (optional)
Green Salad (see below)

ᵛ Warm Vegetable Salad with Summer Herbs

T his warm salad makes a delicious vegetarian starter but can also be served as an accompanying vegetable. The slowly cooked mushrooms give it an intense rustic flavour.

9 ozs (255 g) mushrooms
1 oz (30 g/¼ stick) butter
13 ozs (375 g) carrots
1 teasp. salt
a pinch of sugar
13 ozs (375 g) courgettes
1 pint (600 ml/2½ cups) water
2½ fl ozs (63 ml/generous ¼ cup)
cream
1 teasp. chopped parsley
1 teasp. chopped chives
1 teasp. chopped tarragon
salt and freshly ground pepper

Garnish
sprigs of chervil and chive flowers

Serves 5-6

Slice the mushrooms and stalks finely, melt the butter in a pan, allow it to foam and just as it begins to turn golden add the mushrooms. Cook over a high heat until they brown slightly, then reduce the heat and cook slowly until dark and delicious.

Wash and scrape or thinly peel the carrots, cut into julienne strips ⅛ inch (3 mm) × 2½ inches (6.5 cm) thick approx. Bring 1 pint (600 ml/ 2½ cups) water to a fast rolling boil with the salt and sugar, and cook the carrot juliennes for 4 minutes approx.; drain, refresh under cold water and drain again. Spread out on a plate until needed.

Cut the courgettes into similar-sized julienne strips. Bring another pint of water to the boil and blanch the courgettes in it for 1 minute, refresh and spread out in a single layer like the carrots.

Add the cream to the mushrooms and allow to bubble until most of the cream is absorbed, season with salt and freshly ground pepper. Add the carrot and courgette juliennes and allow to heat gently. Finally stir in the herbs. Arrange on warm plates garnished with sprigs of chervil and chive flowers and serve immediately with crusty bread.

Cruditées with Tapenade

*C*ruditées, *meaning raw vegetables, is one of my favourite starters. It fulfils all my criteria for a first course: small helpings of very crisp vegetables with a good strong mayonnaise. The plates look tempting, taste delicious and, provided you keep the helpings small, are not too filling. Better still it's actually good for you – so you can feel very virtuous instead of feeling pangs of guilt!*

Children also love Cruditées. They may not fancy Tapenade, but you could use other dips such as Garlic Mayonnaise or Sweet Pea Guacamole (see page 99). Cut the vegetables into bite-sized bits so they can be picked up easily. You don't even need knives and forks because they are usually eaten with fingers.

Use as many of the following vegetables as are in season:

very fresh button mushrooms, quartered
very ripe, firm tomatoes quartered *or* left whole with the calyx on if they are freshly picked
purple sprouting broccoli, broken (not cut) into florets
calabrese (green sprouting broccoli), broken into florets
cauliflower, broken into florets
French beans *or* mangetout peas
baby carrots, *or* larger carrots cut into 2-inch (5 cm) sticks
cucumber, cut into 2-inch (5 cm) sticks
tiny spring onions, trimmed
celery, cut into 2-inch (5 cm) sticks
chicory, in leaves
red, green or yellow peppers, seeds removed, cut into 2-inch (5 cm) strips
very fresh Brussels sprouts, cut into halves *or* quarters
whole radishes, with green tops left on
finely chopped parsley
finely chopped thyme
finely chopped chives
sprigs of watercress

Tapenade – see page 76

A typical plate of Cruditées might include the following: 4 sticks of carrot, 2 or 3 sticks of red and green pepper, 2 or 3 sticks of celery, 2 or 3 sticks of cucumber, 1 mushroom cut in quarters, 1 whole radish with a little green leaf left on, 1 tiny tomato or 2 quarters, 1 Brussels sprout cut in quarters, and a little pile of chopped fresh herbs.

Wash and prepare the vegetables. Arrange on individual plates in contrasting colours, with a little bowl of Tapenade or chosen sauce in the centre. Alternatively, fill a large dish or basket for the centre of the table. Pretty edible sauce containers can be made from courgette flowers, hollowed out tomatoes or cucumber.

vv* Tian of Mediterranean Vegetables Baked with Olive Oil and Herbs

3 small aubergines, 1½ lbs (675 g) approx.
6-8 very ripe tomatoes (approx. 2 lbs/900 g), peeled
4-6 courgettes, 1¼ lbs (560 g) approx.
4-6 fl ozs (120-175 ml/½-¾ cup) extra virgin olive oil
4 spring onions, thinly sliced *or* 1 onion very thinly sliced
2-4 teasp. herbs – rosemary, thyme or annual marjoram, chopped
salt and freshly ground pepper

Garnish
1-2 tablesp. freshly chopped parsley

a large shallow dish, 14 × 12 inches (35.5 × 30.5 cm) or 2 dishes, 10 × 8½ inches (25.5 × 21.5 cm)

Serves 8-10

To prepare the vegetables, cut the aubergines into ½ inch (1 cm) slices, sprinkle them with salt and leave to drain for 15-20 minutes. Rinse to remove the excess salt and pat dry with kitchen paper. Peel the tomatoes and cut in thick slices. Slice the courgettes at an angle in ⅜ inch/ 7 mm slices.

Preheat the oven to 200°C/ 400°F/regulo 6. Drizzle a shallow baking dish with half of the olive oil, sprinkle on the thinly sliced spring onion and some chopped herbs, arrange the aubergine slices alternately with tomatoes and courgettes. Season with salt and freshly ground pepper, drizzle with the remaining oil and sprinkle over a little more marjoram.

Bake for 25-30 minutes or until vegetables are cooked through. (Keep an eye on them: you may need to cover with tin foil if they are getting too brown.) Sprinkle with some parsley and serve.

VARIATION
ᵛSprinkle Buttered Crumbs (see page 65) mixed with grated cheese on top and brown under the grill before serving.

v* Rustic Mediterranean Sandwich

Antony Worrall-Thompson, one of London's most creative chefs, has been a trendsetter for many years. This recipe, inspired by one of his creations, is possibly my favourite summer lunch. We do lots of variations depending on what we have to hand.

8 ozs (225 g) aubergines
8 ozs (225 g) courgettes
4 fl ozs (120 ml/½ cup) olive oil
2 red peppers
2 yellow peppers
1 round loaf of Italian country
    bread *or* 2 small 'Schull' loaves
2 cloves of garlic, halved
4 tablesp. (5 American tablesp.)
    Tapenade (see below)
30 large basil leaves
5 ozs (140 g) sundried tomatoes
    in oil (optional)
4 tablesp. (5 American tablesp.)
    Pesto (see page 7)
8 ozs (225 g) Mozzarella cheese
    (di Bufala if possible), thinly
    sliced
2 ozs (55 g) rocket leaves
1 tablesp. balsamic vinegar
salt and freshly ground pepper

Garnish
rocket leaves
cherry tomatoes
4 ozs (110 g) stoned black olives
a little extra virgin olive oil

Serves 8-12

Slice the aubergines and courgettes lengthwise into ¼ inch (5 mm) thick slices. Sprinkle with a little salt, put into a colander and allow to degorge for a few minutes.

Rub the skin of the peppers with a little of the olive oil, put on to a baking sheet and roast in a preheated moderate oven, 180°C/350°F/ regulo 4, for 30-40 minutes or until they collapse and look slightly charred all over. Peel them and remove the seeds.

Rinse the aubergines and courgettes and pat dry with kitchen paper. Heat 1 inch (2.5 cm) approx. of olive oil in a frying pan, cook the aubergine slices until golden on each side and keep aside.

Heat a grill pan, brush the courgette slices with olive oil and cook for a few minutes on each side. Assemble and prepare all the rest of the ingredients.

Cut a lid off the top of the loaf or loaves, hollow out the centre leaving a crust of 1 inch (2.5 cm) approx. all round. Rub the inside of the lid and the loaf/loaves with a cut clove of garlic and brush liberally with olive oil. Spread a layer of Tapenade on the base, then layer the ingredients in the following order, seasoning each layer well with salt and freshly ground pepper: half the aubergines, half the courgettes, red pepper, yellow pepper, basil, chopped sundried tomatoes, sliced Mozzarella cheese, Pesto, remaining courgettes, remaining aubergines, rocket leaves, balsamic vinegar.

Replace the lid and wrap the loaf or loaves with cling film. Put on a large plate, cover with a board and weigh down for several hours or overnight.

The Mediterranean Sandwich can be served at room temperature without being reheated, or you may prefer to put it into a preheated oven, 250°C/475°F/regulo 9, to crisp the outside for 5-10 minutes. Serve cut in wedges or in a cross section, garnished with rocket leaves and cherry tomatoes. Sprinkle with chive flowers if available and perhaps a black olive or two.

TAPENADE

2 ozs (55 g) anchovy fillets
3½ ozs (100 g/½ cup) stoned
   black olives
1 tablesp. (20 g/4 teasp.) capers
1 teasp. Dijon mustard
1 teasp. freshly squeezed lemon
   juice
freshly ground pepper
2-3 tablesp. (37 ml/scant ¼ cup)
   extra virgin olive oil

W hizz up the anchovy fillets for a few seconds (preferably in a food processor) with the stoned black olives, capers, mustard, lemon juice and pepper. Alternatively, use a pestle and mortar. When it becomes a rough purée, add the olive oil.

VV Vegetable Stew with Fresh Spices and Banana and Yoghurt Raita

T his spicy stew tastes even better the day after you make it. Vary the vegetables depending on what you have to hand.

4-8 carrots
2 large parsnips *or* white turnips
4 ozs (110 g) button mushrooms
4 ozs (110 g) cauliflower
3-4 potatoes
2 × 6 inch (15 cm) courgettes,
   green *or* golden
2 stalks broccoli
2 teasp. coriander seeds
2 teasp. cumin seeds
1 teasp. mustard seeds
1 teasp. cardamom seeds
10 whole cloves

3 inch (7.5 cm) piece of
   cinnamon bark
¼ teasp. cayenne pepper
1 teasp. ground turmeric
1 oz (30 g) fresh ginger root
4 cloves of garlic
1 teasp. sugar
4-5 tablesp. approx. olive oil *or*
   clarified butter (see glossary)
2 onions, sliced into rings
3 cups coconut milk (see below)
1 teasp. sea salt
juice of 1 lemon

Garnish
flat parsley or coriander leaves
2½ ozs (70 g/½ cup) roasted
   almonds *or* cashew nuts

Serves 6

First prepare the vegetables. Peel or scrape the carrots and cut them into pieces 1½ inches (4 cm) long approx. If the pieces are very chunky cut them into quarters. Peel and quarter the parsnips, cut out the core and cut into pieces similar to the carrots. Quarter the mushrooms. Break the cauliflower and broccoli into florets. Peel the potatoes and cut into ½ inch (1 cm) cubes.

Grind all the whole spices in a spice grinder, add the turmeric and cayenne. Chop the garlic and ginger and make into a paste either in a pestle and mortar or food processor.

Heat the olive oil or clarified butter in a wide saucepan, add the onion, garlic and ginger, cook over a medium heat until the onion has turned golden brown (6-8 minutes approx.), lower the heat, add the spices and sugar and continue to cook for 3-4 minutes, stirring constantly. Add the carrots, parsnips, coconut milk, lemon juice and sea salt, increase the heat, cover and bring to the boil and simmer for 10 minutes. Add the potatoes and cook until tender.

Meanwhile blanch the cauliflower and broccoli in boiling salted water, remove when almost cooked but still crisp, refresh in cold water, drain and keep aside. Boil the courgettes for 5-6 minutes.

Fry the mushroom quarters in a hot pan in a little olive oil or clarified butter, season with salt and pepper and keep aside. When the potatoes are cooked add the mushrooms, broccoli, thickly sliced courgettes and cauliflower to the stew, cover, allow to bubble up for a minute, taste and correct seasoning. It often needs more salt at this point to enhance the flavour.

Garnish with flat parsley or coriander leaves and roasted almond or cashew nuts. Serve immediately with Ballymaloe Tomato Relish and Banana and Yoghurt Raita (see below). Poppodums are also a nice accompaniment.

Coconut milk: Coconut milk can be bought in tins. Chaokoh is best. Alternatively pour 3 cups of boiling water over 3 cups of dried coconut, leave it to steep for 30 minutes, then put into a liquidiser and blend at high speed for 3 minutes. Pour through a strainer lined with several layers of muslin. Then twist the ends of the muslin and squeeze out every last drop of liquid. Discard the pulp and use the milk.

^V BANANA AND YOGHURT RAITA

3 firm ripe bananas
2 ozs (55 g) approx. raisins *or*
    sultanas
1 oz (30 g/¼ cup) blanched
    slivered almonds
7 fl ozs (200 ml/generous ¾ cup)
    natural yoghurt
3½ fl ozs (90 ml/scant ½ cup)
    cream
3½ fl ozs (90 ml/scant ½ cup)
    sour cream
1 tablesp. approx. pure Irish
    honey
4-6 cardamom pods
pinch of salt

Serves 8-10

P our boiling water over the raisins
or sultanas and leave for
10 minutes. Toast the almonds. Mix
the yoghurt with the creams, add the
honey, taste and add more if needed.
Add the raisins. Remove the seeds
from the cardamom pods, crush in a
pestle and mortar and add to the
mixture. Slice the banana, add to the
yoghurt and season with a pinch of
salt. Turn into a serving bowl and
scatter with toasted almonds. Chill for
1 hour if possible.

^{VV} Indian Spiced Vegetable Pakoras with Mango Relish

N *ibbling crispy vegetable fritters called
Pakoras seems to be a national
pastime in India. This delicious version
comes from* 'The Inspired Vegetarian'
*by Louise Pickford published by Stewart,
Tabori & Chang.*

Vegetables
1 small aubergine, cut into ¼ inch
    (5 mm) slices
1 teasp. salt
2 medium courgettes, cut into
    1 inch (2.5 cm) slices (if they
    are very large quarter them)
12 cauliflower florets
6 large mushrooms, cut in half

Batter
6 ozs (170 g/1⅓ cups) white flour

1 tablesp. chopped fresh
    coriander
1 scant teasp. salt
2 teasp. curry powder
1 tablesp. olive oil
1 tablesp. freshly squeezed lemon
    juice
¾-1 cup cold water

Garnish
lemon wedges
fresh coriander *or* parsley

Serves 4-6

Put the aubergine into a colander,
sprinkle with the salt, and let drain
while preparing the other vegetables.
    Blanch the courgettes and

cauliflower florets separately in boiling salted water for 2 minutes. Drain, refresh under cold water and dry well. Rinse the aubergine and pat dry.

Put the flour, coriander, salt and curry powder into a large bowl. Gradually whisk in the oil, lemon juice and water until the batter is the consistency of thick cream. Heat good quality oil in a deepfrier. Lightly whisk the batter and dip the vegetables into it in batches one by one, then drop them carefully into the hot oil.

Fry the pakoras for 2-3 minutes on each side, turning them with a slotted spoon. Drain on kitchen paper and keep warm in a moderate oven uncovered while you cook the remainder. Allow the oil to come back to 180°C/350°F/regulo 4 between batches.

When all the vegetable fritters are ready, garnish with lemon wedges and fresh coriander or parsley. Serve at once with the Mango Relish.

MANGO RELISH

1 mango, peeled and diced
2 fl ozs (60 ml/¼ cup) medium
   sherry
2 fl ozs (60 ml/¼ cup) water
2 fl ozs (60 ml/¼ cup) white wine
   vinegar
2 tablesp. sugar
½ cinnamon stick
1 star anise
½ teasp. salt
a pinch of ground mace
1 small red pepper, seeded and
   diced
1 tablesp. lemon juice

Put the sherry, water, vinegar, sugar, cinnamon, star anise, salt and mace into a small, heavy-bottomed saucepan. Bring to a boil and simmer over medium heat for 5 minutes. Add the mango, red pepper and lemon juice, lower the heat and simmer for 5 minutes more. Remove from the heat and let cool completely. Spoon into a screw-top jar and refrigerate until required.

ᵛ Courgette and Basil Lasagne

I*f you consider lasagne to be just a technique then you can ring the changes with all manner of fillings. Annual marjoram may be substituted for basil with equally delicious results.*

9 sheets of homemade lasagne
   (see *Simply Delicious in France
   & Italy*, p. 59) or ½ box dried
   lasagne (choose the thinnest
   possible)

**2 lbs (900 g) courgettes, thinly
    sliced and cooked in olive oil
    (see page 50)**
**1¼ pints (750 ml) well seasoned
    Béchamel Sauce (not too
    thick, see page 120)**
**5 ozs (140 g) Parmesan cheese,
    preferably Parmigiano
    Reggiano, freshly grated**
salt and freshly ground pepper
**10-20 basil leaves, depending on
    size**

Serves 6-8

First taste the courgettes and
Béchamel Sauce, making sure they
are delicious and well seasoned.

Blanch the lasagne in boiling
salted water for a minute or so if it is
homemade, and otherwise according
to the directions on the packet.
Spread a little Béchamel Sauce on the
base of a lightly buttered gratin dish,
sprinkle with a little grated Parmesan
cheese, cover with strips of lasagne,
more sauce, a sprinkling of Parmesan,
half the courgettes and a layer of basil
leaves. Next put another layer of

lasagne and repeat the previous layer.
Cover the final layer of lasagne with
sauce and a good sprinkling of
Parmesan cheese. (Make sure all the
lasagne is under the sauce.)

Bake in a preheated moderate
oven, 180°C/350°F/regulo 4, for
10-15 minutes if the lasagne is
homemade, otherwise for 30 minutes
approx. or until golden and bubbly
on top. If possible, leave to stand for
10-15 minutes before cutting to allow
the layers to compact. Serve with a
good green salad.

Resumé
  1. **Béchamel sauce**
  2. **Grated Parmesan**
  3. **Lasagne**
  4. **Béchamel sauce**
  5. **Grated Parmesan**
  6. **Courgettes and basil**
  7. **Lasagne**
  8. **Béchamel sauce**
  9. **Grated Parmesan**
  10. **Courgettes and basil**
  11. **Lasagne**
  12. **Béchamel sauce**
  13. **Grated Parmesan**

Mushrooms

Mushroom Soup
vv* Mushroom and Caramelised Onion Salad
v* Stuffed Mushrooms
v* Mushroom Crostini with Rocket and Parmesan
v Mushroom and Thyme Leaf Tart
Risotto with Mushrooms
v* Mushroom Filos
* Chicken Breasts with Mushrooms and Rosemary

We live in exciting times as far as mushrooms are concerned. Not so long ago, buttons were the only mushrooms to be found anywhere. Now, many supermarkets are selling six or seven different kinds – buttons, several sizes of flats, brown mushrooms (which have a more pronounced flavour), oyster mushrooms and the delicious Chinese shitake mushrooms. What riches! We have had great fun recently growing oyster mushrooms in a bag of compost★ in the potting shed. We can pick them off as we want them, and the compost is scattered over the garden when the mushroom-growing is finished. These oyster mushrooms are delicious fried in a little butter and served on toast, or with a steak. As with many other varieties of mushroom, their flavour develops if they are kept for a day or two – worth doing unless you are serving them raw in a salad, in which case they must be absolutely fresh.

There are two foolproof ways of dealing with mushrooms. The first is to cook them very quickly on a hot pan. The second, oddly enough, is to do the exact opposite, and cook them very slowly over a low heat. As the juices which are released early on in the cooking evaporate, the flavour intensifies wonderfully, so that ordinary mushrooms end up tasting almost like wild mushrooms!

★Supplied by Dermot O'Morchoe, Killeen, Kildermot, Gorey, Co. Wexford, Tel: 055-20329.

Mushroom Soup

This recipe was first published in Simply Delicious 2 *but it deserves a place here also, because it's one of the* fastest of all soups to make and a great favourite. Mushroom Soup *is best made with flat mushrooms or button mushrooms a few days old, which have developed a slightly stronger flavour.*

1 lb (450 g/5 cups) mushrooms
4 ozs (110 g/1 cup) onions
1½ ozs (45 g/⅜ stick) butter
1 oz (30 g/scant ¼ cup) flour
salt and freshly ground pepper
1 pint (600 ml/2½ cups) milk
1 pint (600 ml/2½ cups)
     homemade chicken stock

Chop the onions finely. Melt the butter in a saucepan on a gentle heat. Toss the onions in it, cover and sweat until soft and completely cooked.

Meanwhile, chop up the mushrooms very finely.* Add to the saucepan and cook on a high heat for 3-4 minutes. Now stir in the flour, cook on a low heat for 2-3 minutes, season with salt and freshly ground pepper, then add the stock and milk gradually, stirring all the time. Increase the heat and bring to the boil. Taste, add a dash of cream if necessary and serve.

*If you can't be bothered to chop the mushrooms finely, just slice them and then whizz the soup in a liquidiser for a few seconds when it is cooked.

ᵛᵛ* Mushroom and Caramelised Onion Salad

T his salad may be part of a Plate of Garden Salads (see page 71) or it could be served just as an accompaniment to cold meats or poached salmon.

12 ozs (340 g/6 cups) mushrooms
2 large onions, sliced
2 tablesp. approx. olive oil
salt and freshly ground pepper
1 large clove of garlic, crushed
freshly squeezed lemon juice

Serves 6-8

Heat a little of the olive oil in a heavy -bottomed saucepan and cook the onions gently over a low heat. Stir

every few minutes so that they brown evenly. This operation may take 20-30 minutes and is vital to the success of the salad. The onions should be slightly caramelised in oil.

Meanwhile, thinly slice the mushrooms and sauté on a hot pan. Season each batch with salt and freshly ground pepper, a very little crushed garlic and a squeeze of lemon juice. Add the onions to the mushrooms as soon as they are cooked and taste. Correct the seasoning if necessary.

Like most salads this is best served at room temperature.

v* Stuffed Mushrooms

Wasn't it Shirley Conran who first said 'Life is too short to stuff a mushroom'? Well, try these – they are completely delicious as a starter, as an accompanying vegetable or even as a garnish, and are worth every minute.

approx. 8 flat mushrooms

Filling
**4 ozs (110 g/1¼ cups)
  mushrooms, chopped
2 tablesp. (2 American tablesp. +
  2 teasp.) white breadcrumbs
1 tablesp. approx. melted butter
1 egg yolk
1-2 teasp. cream
1-2 teasp. chopped chives
1-2 teasp. chopped parsley
1 clove of garlic, crushed
salt and freshly ground pepper**

Coating
**4-8 fl ozs (120-250 ml/½-1 cup)
  Béchamel Sauce (see page 120)
2 ozs (55 g/½ cup) Buttered
  Crumbs (twice recipe on
  page 65)
1½ ozs (45 g/⅜ cup) Irish
  Cheddar cheese, grated**

Arrange the flat mushrooms in a single layer in an ovenproof serving dish or dishes. Mix all the ingredients for the filling together, season the flat mushrooms and divide the filling between them. Spread a little sauce over each one and top with a mixture of grated cheese and Buttered Crumbs.*

Bake in a preheated oven, 200°C/400°F/regulo 6, for 15 minutes approx. The tops should be lightly browned. Flash under the grill if necessary.

*May be prepared ahead to this point.

v* Mushroom Crostini with Rocket and Parmesan

This is a poshed up version of mushrooms on toast. Virtually all fungi are delicious on toast so this can be very humble or very exotic depending on the variety chosen.

**4-6 flat mushrooms *or* large
  oyster mushrooms
2 slices of Shull loaf *or* a large
  good quality baguette**

**extra virgin olive oil
marjoram, thyme *or* rosemary
1 clove of garlic (optional)
rocket leaves
freshly grated Parmesan cheese,
  preferably Parmigiano
  Reggiano**

Serves 2

Heat 1 inch (2.5 cm) approx. of olive oil in a frying pan until just below smoking point. Fry the pieces of bread one at a time, whip them out just as soon as they become golden, drain on kitchen paper and keep warm. (The oil may be strained and used again for another purpose.)

Heat a little olive oil, or olive oil and butter, in a frying pan. Remove the stalks from the mushrooms and place them skin-side down on the pan in a single layer, put a little dot of butter into each one or better still use garlic or marjoram butter. That is made quite simply by mixing chopped garlic and parsley or annual marjoram into a little butter. Alternatively, sprinkle with freshly chopped marjoram and some crushed garlic if you like. Season with salt and freshly ground pepper.

Cook first on one side (the length of time will depend on the size of the mushroom: it could be anything from 3-6 minutes), then turn over as soon as you notice that the gills are covered with droplets of juice. Cook on the other side until tender.

Meanwhile, rub the surface of the warm crostini with a cut clove of garlic, and put them on 2 hot plates. Arrange a few fresh rocket leaves on each one and top with overlapping mushrooms. Sprinkle with a little freshly grated Parmesan cheese and serve immediately. If there are any buttery juices in the pan, spoon every drop over the mushrooms for extra deliciousness.

ᵛ Mushroom and Thyme Leaf Tart

*T*his is a really flavoursome tart – one of the few that tastes super warm or cold. Buy your Parmesan cheese, preferably Parmigiano Reggiano, in a piece if at all possible, because ready-grated cheese is frequently rancid and may spoil the recipe. May I respectfully suggest that you use cream! Both the flavour and texture are quite different if you substitute milk.

8 ozs (225 g) mushrooms, flats if possible
6 ozs (170 g) Rich Shortcrust Pastry (see page 122)
½ oz (15 g/1 tablesp.) butter

1 teasp. fresh thyme leaves
8 fl ozs (250 ml/1 cup) cream
2 eggs and 1 egg yolk, free-range if possible
2 ozs (55 g/½ cup) freshly grated Parmesan cheese, preferably Parmigiano Reggiano
sea salt
freshly ground black pepper
a good pinch of cayenne

a 7 inch (18 cm) flan ring *or* tin with pop up base

Serves 6

Roll out the pastry thinly and line the flan ring or tin. Cover with kitchen paper and fill with baking beans. Bake blind for 15-20 minutes in a preheated moderate oven, 180°C/ 350°F/ regulo 4.

Chop the mushrooms finely, melt the butter and fry the mushrooms on a very high heat. Add thyme leaves and season with salt and freshly ground pepper. Drain well and allow to cool.

Whisk the cream with the eggs and the extra egg yolk, stir in the mushrooms and most of the Parmesan cheese. Taste, add the pinch of cayenne and more seasoning if necessary. Pour into the prebaked pastry case. Sprinkle with the remainder of the grated cheese. Bake in a moderate oven for 30-40 minutes approx. or until the filling is set and the top delicately brown.

Serve with a green salad. Tiny mushroom quiches may be served straight from the oven as appetisers before dinner.

Risotto with Mushrooms

Risotto is often considered to be a sort of dustbin to use up left-overs. Nothing, in fact, could be further from the truth. A perfectly cooked risotto made with proper Carnaroli or Arborio rice is a feast. The technique is altogether different from that used for Indian pilaffs, and for perfection risotto should be served the minute it is cooked.

8 ozs (225 g/4 cups) mushrooms, sliced
14 ozs (400 g/scant 2 cups) Carnaroli or Arborio rice
2 ozs (55 g/½ stick) butter
1¾-2¼ pints (1-1.3 L/4½-5½ cups) broth, chicken stock or vegetable stock
2 tablesp. approx. olive oil
1 onion, finely chopped

2 ozs (55 g/½ cup) freshly grated Parmesan cheese, preferably Parmigiano Reggiano
sea salt

Serves 6

Melt half the butter and just as it foams add in the mushrooms, season with salt and freshly ground pepper, reduce the heat and cook long and slowly until the mushrooms are dark and concentrated in flavour. This method of cooking mushrooms transforms their flavour and makes them taste like wild mushrooms.

Bring the broth or stock to the boil, turn down the heat and keep it simmering. Melt the remaining butter in a heavy-bottomed saucepan with the oil, add the onion and sweat over a gentle heat for 4-5 minutes, until soft but not coloured. Add the rice and stir until well coated (so far the technique is the same as for a pilaff and this is where people become confused). Cook for a minute or so and then add ¼ pint (150 ml/ generous ½ cup) of broth.

Continue to cook in this way stirring continuously. The heat should be brisk, but on the one hand if it is too hot the rice will be soft outside but still chewy inside, and if it is too slow, the rice will be gluey. It is difficult to know which is worse, so the trick is to regulate the heat so that the rice bubbles continuously. The risotto should take 25-30 minutes approx. to cook.

When it has been cooking for 20 minutes approx. add in the cooked mushrooms and from there on add the broth approx. 4 tablespoons at a time. The risotto is done when the rice is cooked but is still ever so slightly *al dente*. It should be soft and creamy and quite loose, rather than thick. The moment you are happy with the texture, stir in the remaining butter and Parmesan cheese, taste and add more salt if necessary. Serve immediately. Risotto should not hang about!

ᵛ* Mushroom Filos

F ilo pastry can be used to make tasty little mouthfuls of different shapes.

filo pastry
melted butter
Mushroom à la Crème
    (see opposite)

Defrost the filo pastry if necessary, and unfold it.

For parcels: Brush the top sheet with melted butter, put 1-2 tablespoons of the mushroom filling in the centre of the sheet, 2½ inches (6.5 cm) approx. in from the edge, fold the pastry over the filling and then fold in the edges, roll over and over to enclose the filling. Brush with egg wash and melted butter. Bake in a preheated oven, 200°C/400°F/ regulo 6, for 15-20 minutes. Serve as a canapé, starter or main course depending on size.

For triangles: Cut each sheet in 4 lengthwise, brush each strip with melted butter, put a heaped teaspoon of filling near the end of the strip, fold over and over from side to side to form a triangle. Brush with melted butter and egg wash, and bake as above.

V MUSHROOM À LA CRÈME

8 ozs (225 g/2¼ cups)
    mushrooms, sliced
½-1 oz (15-30 g/⅛-¼ stick) butter
3 ozs (85 g/¾ cup) onions, finely
    chopped
1 clove of garlic, crushed
    (optional)
salt and freshly ground pepper
squeeze of lemon juice
4 fl ozs (120 ml/½ cup) cream
freshly chopped parsley
½ tablesp. freshly chopped chives
    (optional)

Melt the butter in a heavy saucepan until it foams. Add the chopped onions, crushed garlic if liked, cover and sweat on a gentle heat for 5-10 minutes or until quite soft but not coloured; remove the onions to a bowl. Increase the heat and cook the sliced mushrooms, in batches if necessary. Season each batch with salt, freshly ground pepper and a tiny squeeze of lemon juice. Add the onions to the mushrooms in the saucepan, then add the cream and allow to bubble for a few minutes. Taste and correct the seasoning, and add parsley and chives if used.

Note: Mushroom à la Crème may be served as a vegetable, or as a filling for vols au vent, bouchées or pancakes. It may be used as an enrichment for casseroles and stews or, by adding a little more cream or stock, may be served as a sauce with beef, lamb, chicken or veal.

Mushroom à la Crème keeps well in the fridge for 4-5 days.

* Chicken Breasts with Mushrooms and Rosemary

Soaking the chicken breasts in milk gives them a tender and moist texture. We often serve this recipe with orzo, a pasta which looks like grains of rice and is all the rage in our house these days.

4 chicken breasts, free-range if
    possible
milk (optional)
salt and freshly ground pepper
½ oz (15 g/⅛ stick) butter
2 tablesp. approx. chopped
    shallot *or* spring onion

4 ozs (110 g/2 cups) mushrooms,
    sliced
¼ pint (150 ml/generous ½ cup)
    homemade chicken stock
¼ pint (150 ml/generous ½ cup)
    cream
2 small sprigs of rosemary
1 dessertsp. chopped parsley

Garnish
sprigs of rosemary and parsley
orzo (optional – see below)

Serves 4

Soak the chicken breasts in milk — just enough to cover them — for 1 hour approx. Discard the milk, dry with kitchen paper, and season with salt and pepper. Heat the butter in a sauté pan until foaming, put in the chicken breasts and turn them in the butter; add a sprig of rosemary, and cover with a round of greaseproof paper and the lid. Cook on a gentle heat for 5-7 minutes or until just barely cooked.

Meanwhile sweat the shallots gently in a pan in a little butter, add the sliced mushrooms, season with salt and freshly ground pepper and keep aside.

When the chicken breasts are cooked, remove them to a plate and discard the sprig of rosemary. Add the chicken stock and cream to the saucepan with a fresh sprig of rosemary. Reduce the liquid by half over a medium heat; this will thicken the sauce slightly and intensify the flavour. When you are happy with the flavour and texture of the sauce, add the chicken breasts and the mushroom mixture back in, simmer for 1-2 minutes, taste and correct the seasoning. Serve immediately, garnished with sprigs of fresh rosemary and parsley, with some freshly cooked orzo as an accompaniment.

Orzo with Fresh Herbs

O*rzo looks like fat grains of rice but is in fact made from semolina.*

7 ozs (200 g/1 cup) orzo
2 pints (1.1 L/5 cups) water
1½ teasp. salt
½-1 oz (15–30 g/⅛-¼ stick) butter
salt and freshly ground pepper

Garnish
chopped parsley (optional)

Serves 4

Bring the water to a fast rolling boil and add the salt. Sprinkle in the orzo, cook for 5-6 minutes or until just cooked. Drain, rinse under hot water and toss with the butter. Season with freshly ground pepper and mix in the chopped parsley.

Onions and Garlic

^{vv*} *Onions Monégasque*
^{v*} *Roast Onions with Marjoram or Garlic Butter*
^{v*} *Onion Bhajis with Tomato and Chilli Sauce*
[*] *Pissaladière*
Greek Lamb, Onion and Butter Bean Stew
^v *Onion Sauce (Sauce Soubise)*
^{vv*} *Roast Garlic*

Every cuisine in the world seems to use onions in some shape or form, and I can't imagine life without them. In Ireland they are probably the most taken for granted of all vegetables, but occasionally they should be allowed to star in their own right. They have many different flavours, depending on how they are cooked. There are also many varieties – spring onions, scallions, shallots, perennial Welsh onions, huge Spanish onions and the latest trendy addition suddenly sprouting up in all the vegetable shops, the sweet, mild, red onions that are so useful for salads and Mediterranean dishes.

As onions are relatively cheap and very widely available, many gardeners don't feel inclined to devote precious space to them – but there are some people for whom a well saved crop, dangling from the rafters of the potting shed, is a perennial pride and joy.

As for garlic, we've certainly taken to it like nobody's business! Few Irish kitchens, I suspect, are without a few cloves of garlic these days, and that definitely wouldn't have been the case 20 years ago – although interestingly there are frequent references to garlic in old Irish manuscripts, indicating that it is not as new an addition to our national cuisine as we might think. Garlic can pep up food in so many ways, and impart a different flavour each time depending on whether it is crushed, chopped or cooked whole. Besides being delicious it's extremely healthy. Why bother to resort to garlic pills when you can use it in cooking and enjoy it?

^{vv*} Onions Monégasque

This gutsy salad from Monaco keeps for not just days but weeks, and is delicious with cold meat or game or as part of a salad plate.

1 lb (450 g) button onions,
  scallions, young summer
  onions *or* leeks★
12 fl ozs (350 ml/1½ cups) water
4 fl ozs (120 ml/½ cup) white
  vinegar
1 tablesp. (1¼ American tablesp.)
  olive oil
2 tablesp. (2½ American tablesp.)
  sugar
8 fl ozs (250 ml/1 cup)
  homemade Tomato Purée
  (see below) *or* 2 tablesp. (2½
  American tablesp.) tomato
  paste mixed with 8 fl ozs
  (250 ml/1 cup) water
½ bay leaf
½ teasp. thyme leaves
sprig of parsley
3 ozs (85 g/½ cup) seedless raisins
salt and freshly ground pepper

Serves 6 approx.

*This recipe can also be made with larger onions if they are cut lengthwise so that each segment has a piece of root left on, which will hold the leaves together.

Simply put all the ingredients into a saucepan, cover and stew gently until the onions are soft – anything from 20 minutes to 2 hours. Button onions take 2 hours approx. Remove the lid after the first hour. Serve cold.

Note: We also use young Japanese onions in spring for this recipe. We cook them whole with 3-4 inches (7.5-10 cm) of the green shoot left on.

TOMATO PURÉE
2 lbs (900 g) very ripe tomatoes
2 teasp. sugar
a good pinch of salt
a few twists of black pepper
1 small onion, chopped

Cut the tomatoes into quarters and put into a stainless steel saucepan with the onion, salt, freshly ground pepper and sugar. Cook on a gentle heat until the tomatoes are soft (no water is needed). Put through the fine blade of a mouli-légumes or a nylon sieve.

Allow to get cold, refrigerate or freeze.

Note: Tomato Purée is one of the very best ways of preserving the flavour of ripe summer tomatoes for winter. Use for soups, stews, casseroles etc.

ᵛ* Roast Onions with Marjoram or Garlic Butter

S o utterly simple and delicious! Roast onions were one of the big hits in my book Simply Delicious Food for Family & Friends. Here we serve them with Marjoram or Garlic Butter. Eat them on their own or as an accompaniment.

Choose small, medium or large-sized onions. Preheat the oven to 200°C/400°F/regulo 6. Cook the unpeeled onions on a baking tray until soft: this can take anything from 10 minutes to 1 hour depending on size. Serve in their jackets.

To eat, cut off the root end. If they are tiny, squeeze out the onion and enjoy with Marjoram or Garlic Butter and sea salt. Larger onions are best split in half and served with a blob of Marjoram or Garlic Butter melting in the centre. They taste so exquisite that you won't want anything else for supper!

MARJORAM BUTTER

Add 1 tablespoon of chopped annual marjoram to 2 ozs (55 g/½ stick) of butter. Roll into butter pats or form into a roll and wrap in greaseproof paper or tin foil, screwing each end so that it looks like a cracker. Refrigerate to harden.

GARLIC BUTTER

2 ozs (55 g/½ stick) butter
4 teasp. finely chopped parsley
2-3 cloves of garlic, crushed

Cream the butter and stir in the parsley. Add the crushed garlic. Then proceed as for Marjoram Butter.

ᵛ* Onion Bhajis with Tomato and Chilli Sauce

C heap, cheerful and delicious – ideal pub grub!

4 onions, thinly sliced
4 ozs (110 g) white flour
2 teasp. baking powder
1 teasp. chilli powder
2 eggs, beaten
¼ pint (150 ml/generous ½ cup) water
2 tablesp. approx. snipped fresh chives
oil for deepfrying

TOMATO AND CHILLI SAUCE
1 oz (30 g) green chillies, deseeded and chopped (2-3 depending on size)
1 red pepper, deseeded and cut in ¼ inch (5 mm) dice
½ × 14 oz (400 g) tin chopped tomatoes
1 clove of garlic, crushed
1 dessertsp. castor sugar
1 dessertsp. soft brown sugar
1 tablesp. (1 American tablesp. + 1 teasp.) white wine vinegar

**2 tablesp. (2½ American tablesp.)
    water**
salt and freshly ground pepper

First make the sauce. Put the chillies, pepper, tomatoes and garlic into a stainless steel saucepan with the sugar, vinegar and water. Season and simmer for 10 minutes until reduced by half.

Sieve the flour, baking powder and chilli powder into a bowl. Make a well in the centre, add the eggs, gradually add in the water and mix to make a smooth batter. Stir in the thinly sliced onions and chives. Season well with salt and freshly ground pepper.

Just before serving, heat the oil to 170°C/340°F. Fry dessertspoons of the batter for 5 minutes approx. on each side until crisp and golden, then drain on kitchen paper. Serve hot with the Tomato and Chilli Sauce.

* Pissaladière

T his is a French version of a pizza, usually made with a white yeast bread base but also delicious with a rich shortcrust. Serve as an appetiser, starter or a main course.

Pastry base
**12 ozs (340 g) shortcrust pastry
    made with:**
**8 ozs (225 g/generous 1½ cups)
    flour**
4 ozs (110 g/1 stick) butter
water to bind

Filling
2 lbs (900 g) onions, thinly sliced
**3 tablesp. (4 American tablesp.)
    olive oil**
2 sprigs of thyme
2 sprigs of rosemary
a few basil leaves
2 sprigs of parsley

**salt, freshly ground pepper and
    sugar**
**1-2 tins anchovy fillets, drained
    and halved lengthwise**
**2-3 ozs (55-85 g) black olives
    (Niçoise for preference)**

**Swiss roll tin, 9 × 12 inches
    (23 × 30.5 cm)**

Serves 6-8 as a main course

Line the Swiss roll tin with the shortcrust pastry, prick the base with a fork, line with kitchen paper, fill with baking beans and bake blind in a preheated moderate oven, 180°C/350°F/regulo 4, for 15-20 minutes.

Heat the olive oil in a pan large enough to take all the onions. Add the sliced onions, herbs and a little salt, pepper and sugar. Cover tightly and sweat gently over a low heat for 30 minutes approx. until the onions are meltingly tender. Discard the herb sprigs. Cool slightly.

Spread the melted onions thickly on the pastry base, arrange the anchovy fillets in a lattice on top and place an olive in the centre of each diamond. (Remove the stones if you like but I usually don't bother.) Increase the heat to 200°C/400°F/ regulo 6. Bake for 20-25 minutes or until brown and bubbly. Serve cut into squares – hot, warm or cold.

Greek Lamb, Onion and Butter Bean Stew

I *ate this Greek version of Irish stew over a wine shop in Thessaloniki. It was comforting and delicious after a long day.*

2½ lb (1.15 kg) shoulder of lamb, cut into 1½ inch (4 cm) cubes
1½ lbs (.75 kg) baby onions, peeled
8 ozs (225 g/1⅓ cups) butter beans
3-4 tablesp. (4-5 American tablesp.) extra virgin olive oil
6 whole cloves garlic, peeled
2 bay leaves
generous sprig thyme
½-¾ pint (300-450 ml/1¼-1½ cups) homemade lamb *or* chicken stock
1 teasp. salt
freshly ground pepper

Garnish
coarsely chopped parsley

Serves 6

Day before: Cover the butter beans with plenty of cold water and leave to soak overnight.

Next day: Heat the olive oil in a pan. Toss the meat, onions and garlic cloves in batches in the hot pan and transfer to a casserole. Drain the butter beans and add with 2 bay leaves and a large sprig of thyme. Pour in the stock – it should come about half way up the meat. Add the salt, bring to the boil, cover and simmer for 1 hour approx. or until all the ingredients are tender. Taste, because it may need more seasoning.

The stew ought to be nice and juicy but if there is altogether more juice than is necessary or if it is a little weak, strain off the liquid and reduce to the required strength and quantity in a wide uncovered pan. Add the meat, onions and butter beans back in. Reheat. Sprinkle with coarsely chopped parsley and serve.

^v Onion Sauce (Sauce Soubise)

O*nion Sauce is absolutely wonderful with roast lamb. It is a sort of forgotten flavour which makes a delicious change from the more usual mint jelly.*

6 onions, thinly sliced or finely
    chopped
4 ozs (110 g/1 stick) butter
1 teasp. salt
1 teasp. sugar
½ teasp. freshly ground pepper
1 tablesp. approx. flour

1 pint (600 ml/2½ cups) milk *or*
    ¾ pint (450 ml/2 cups) milk
    and ¼ pint (150 ml/generous
    ½ cup) cream

Serves 8-10

Sweat the onions in the butter until really soft but not coloured. Season with salt, sugar and freshly ground pepper.

    Stir in the flour, add the milk or milk and cream, bring to the boil and simmer gently for a further 5 minutes.

^{vv*} Roast Garlic

E*specially for demon garlic lovers!*

4 medium heads of garlic
sprig of thyme
sprig of rosemary
salt and freshly ground pepper
extra virgin olive oil
water
4 crostini cooked in olive oil
    (see page 83)

Serves 4

Put the heads of garlic into a small, round, ovenproof dish, add the herbs. Season with salt and freshly ground pepper, add a little water and a good drizzle of olive oil. Cover the dish with tin foil and bake in a preheated oven, 160°C/325°F/regulo 3, for 1-1½ hours, depending on the size of the bulbs.

    Serve one bulb per portion on crispy crostini. Each person can squeeze out the garlic and spread it on their bread.

Parsnips

ᵛ Fennel and Parsnip Soup
ᵛᵛ Pan-roasted Parsnips
ᵛ Saratoga Chips
* Parsnip Cakes with Crispy Bacon
ᵛ Potato, Parsnip and Parsley Colcannon

I can never understand why the parsnip, one of my winter favourites, is so widely scorned – but I take comfort from the fact that the much maligned parsnip is making its appearance (with swede turnips and cabbage) on the menus of many of London's most fashionable restaurants. If you have only had parsnips boiled, do try them roasted (my family's passion) or deepfried in thin strips to serve over warm winter salads, or even raw in a grated carrot and parsnip salad.

If you buy them rather than grow your own, try to find unwashed parsnips because very often a bleach which we'd be better off without is used in the washing process.

ᵛ Fennel and Parsnip Soup

An unexpectedly delicious combination of winter flavours guaranteed to convert the most ardent parsnip haters.

1 lb (450 g) parsnips, washed, peeled and cut into ¼ inch (5 mm) dice
2 ozs (55 g/½ stick) butter
1 lb (450 g) bulb fennel, cut into ¼ inch (5 mm) dice
1 onion, diced
salt and freshly ground pepper
2 pints (1.1 L/5 cups) homemade chicken *or* vegetable stock
4 fl ozs (120 ml/¼ cup) milk
4 fl ozs (120 ml/¼ cup) cream

Garnish
finely chopped herb fennel *or* bulb fennel tops

Serves 8

Melt the butter and toss the diced parsnips, fennel and onion in it. Season with salt and freshly ground pepper. Cover and cook on a gentle heat for 10–15 minutes or until soft but not coloured. Add the stock and simmer for 20 minutes. Add the milk and cream. Liquidise or purée in a food processor, taste for seasoning. Serve in a soup tureen sprinkled with finely chopped herb fennel or the tops of the fennel bulb.

^{vv} Pan-roasted Parsnips

I have a real passion for pan-roasted parsnips – we eat them three or four times a week during the parsnip season.

4 parsnips
olive oil
salt and freshly ground pepper

Serves 6-8

Peel the parsnips and cut them into quarters – the chunks should be quite large. Roast in olive oil in a hot oven, 230°C/450°F/regulo 8, turning them frequently so that they do not become too crusty. We often roast them in the same pan as Rustic Roast Potatoes (see *Simply Delicious Food for Family & Friends*, p. 62). Cooked this way they will be crisp outside and soft in the centre.

^v Saratoga Chips

Parsnips also make very good chips. Cook them in good quality oil at 180°C/350°F/regulo 4.

[*] Parsnip Cakes with Crispy Bacon

The basis of this recipe is simply mashed parsnips which we make into parsnip cakes and serve with crispy bacon.

1 lb (450 g) parsnips
1-2 ozs (30-55 g/¼-½ stick)
   butter
salt and freshly ground pepper
seasoned flour
1 beaten egg
white breadcrumbs
olive oil for frying
streaky bacon cut into ¼ inch
   (5 mm) lardons and fried until
   crisp in a little oil

Serves 6

Peel the parsnips thinly with a swivel top peeler, cut into small chunks and cook in boiling salted water until soft. Mash with the butter, season with salt and freshly ground pepper and taste. Wet your hands and shape the mixture into 6 cakes. Dip each in flour, beaten egg and breadcrumbs.

Heat a little olive oil with some butter in a wide frying pan and fry the cakes on a gentle heat until golden on both sides. Serve hot with lardons of crispy bacon or as an accompaniment to a main course.

Roast Red Pepper, Lentil and Goat's Cheese Salad

Pork, Spinach and Herb Terrine

Sweetcorn with Butter and Sea Salt

Salmon with Tomato, Ginger and Fresh Coriander

Red and Yellow Tomato Salad with Basil

^vPotato, Parsnip and Parsley Colcannon

Several Dubliners have waxed lyrical to me about a parsnip colcannon that their Mammy used to make. Here is my version which is a big hit in Cork at any rate!

2 lbs (900 g) parsnips
1 lb (450 g) 'old' potatoes –
    Golden Wonders *or* Kerr's
    Pinks
8-10 fl ozs (250-300 ml/1-1¼
    cups) approx. creamy milk
2 tablesp. approx. chopped
    scallion
salt and freshly ground pepper
2 ozs (55 g/½ stick) approx.
    butter
2 tablesp. approx. chopped
    parsley

Serves 8 approx.

Scrub the potatoes, put them in a saucepan of cold water, add a good pinch of salt and bring to the boil. When the potatoes are about half cooked (15 minutes approx. for 'old' potatoes) strain off two-thirds of the water, replace the lid on the saucepan, put on a gentle heat and allow the potatoes to steam until they are cooked.

Peel the parsnips, cut into chunks and cook in boiling salted water until soft. Drain, mash and keep warm.

When the potatoes are just cooked, put on the milk and bring to the boil with the scallions. Pull the peel off the potatoes, mash quickly while they are still warm and beat in enough boiling milk to make a fluffy purée. (If you have a large quantity, put the potatoes in the bowl of a food mixer and beat with the spade.) Then add in the mashed parsnip with the chopped parsley and the butter and taste for seasoning. Cover with tin foil while reheating so that it doesn't get crusty on top.

Colcannon may be prepared ahead and reheated later in a moderate oven, 180°C/350°F/ regulo 4, for 20-25 minutes approx.

Serve in a hot dish with a lump of butter melting in the centre.

Peas

*v** Garden Peas with Fresh Mint*
*v** Green Pea Soup with Fresh Mint Cream*
vv Sweet Pea Guacamole
** Penne with Fresh Salmon and Garden Peas*
v Sugar Peas or Snow Peas

We have guests who are so bowled over by the pleasures of our home-grown peas in Ballymaloe that they insist we send them a fax every summer the minute the peas have begun to swell in their pods. They drop everything, fly over from London and gorge themselves on peas – both at the table and even in the fields!

The sad fact is that in most shops now, no amount of money can buy you really fresh peas. Once they're picked, peas lose their exquisite sweetness within a few hours, so if you want to eat them at the peak of perfection there's nothing for it but to grow your own. Here again, I have discovered that there is an extra bonus for the gardener, because the tender young pea shoots are delicious in salads, and the peas can be eaten at every stage. Some of the very young pods, if they are growing in abundance, can be harvested, treated like sugar peas and eaten whole. At the other end of the season, when the peas are past their best, leave them on the plants to dry out and harvest them as marrowfats. Then you can make your very own mushy peas in the winter! If you can't bear to waste a morsel, use the pods of the perfect peas to make a pea pod soup, using the basic soup technique.

v* Garden Peas with Fresh Mint

Really fresh peas from the garden are so exquisite that it is difficult to resist eating them all raw as you pod them!

1 lb (450 g) garden peas *or* petits pois, freshly shelled
¼ pint (150 ml/generous ½ cup) water

1 teasp. salt
1 teasp. sugar
sprig of mint
1 oz (30 g/¼ stick) approx. butter
1-2 teasp. freshly chopped mint

Serves 8-10

Bring the water to the boil, add the salt, sugar, mint and the peas. Bring back to the boil and simmer until the peas are cooked – 4-5 minutes. Strain, reserving the water for soup or gravy. Add the butter and a little freshly chopped mint and a little extra seasoning if necessary. Eat immediately.

ᵛ* Green Pea Soup with Fresh Mint Cream

This soup tastes of summer. If you are making it with fresh peas, use the pods to make a vegetable stock and use that as a basis for your soup. Best quality frozen peas also make a delicious soup. Either way be careful not to overcook it!

1½ lbs (675 g) podded peas, fresh *or* frozen
1 oz (30 g) lean ham *or* bacon
½ oz (15 g/1 tablesp.) butter
2 medium spring onions, chopped
outside leaves of a head of lettuce, shredded
sprig of mint
1½ pints (900 ml/3¾ cups) light homemade chicken stock *or* water
salt, freshly ground pepper and sugar
2 tablesp. approx. thick cream

Garnish
whipped cream
freshly chopped mint

Serves 6-8

Cut the ham into very fine shreds. Melt the butter and sweat the ham for 5 minutes approx., add the spring onions and cook for another 1-2 minutes. Then add the peas, lettuce, mint and the light chicken stock or water. Season with salt, pepper and sugar. Bring to the boil with the lid off and cook for 5 minutes approx. until the peas are just tender.

Liquidise and add a little cream to taste. Serve hot or chilled with a blob of whipped cream mixed with some freshly chopped mint.

If this soup is made ahead, reheat uncovered and serve immediately. It will lose its fresh taste and bright lively colour if it sits in a bain marie or simmers at length in a pot.

ᵛᵛ Sweet Pea Guacamole

I came across this combination in California served on tiny warm tortillas, but little pancakes are also very good and easier to make!

1 lb (450 g) podded fresh *or* frozen peas
2 tablesp. (2 American tablesp. + 2 teasp.) extra virgin olive oil

2 tablesp. (2 American tablesp. +
   2 teasp.) freshly squeezed lime
   juice
2 tablesp. approx. chopped
   parsley
2 tablesp. approx. fresh coriander,
   finely chopped
½ fresh chilli, finely chopped
   (seeds removed)
¼ teasp. ground cumin
½ teasp. ground coriander
½ teasp. approx. salt

Garnish
blobs of crème fraîche *or* thick
   natural yoghurt (optional)

Serves 6

Cook the peas in boiling salted water for 3-4 minutes. Refresh under cold water and drain. Whizz the olive oil with the lime juice, parsley, fresh coriander and chilli in a food processor, blend for 1 minute. Add the peas, cumin, ground coriander and salt and blend until almost smooth. Put into a bowl and serve.

Serve on tiny hot pancakes, blinis or tortillas with a blob of crème fraîche or thick yoghurt if liked. This guacamole even tastes delicious on a slice of hot crispy toast.

* Penne with Fresh Salmon and Garden Peas

S*anford Allen, a charismatic American violinist and friend, gave me this fresh-tasting pasta recipe.*

8 ozs (225 g) penne
8 ozs (225 g) fresh salmon
1 tablesp. approx. extra virgin
   olive oil
1-2 cloves of garlic, finely
   chopped
8 ozs (225 g/2¼ cups) peas,
   preferably fresh from the
   garden, but good quality
   frozen peas also work quite
   well
2 tablesp. (2 American tablesp. +
   2 teasp.) extra virgin olive oil
½ oz (15 g/1 American tablesp.)
   butter

freshly squeezed juice of ½ lemon
1-2 tablesp. approx. chopped
   parsley

Garnish
extra chopped parsley

Serves 4

Cook the penne in boiling salted water, using 2 tablesp. (2 American tablesp. + 2 teasp.) salt to 4 pints (2.3 L/10 cups) water, for 15-20 minutes approx. Blanch the peas.

Skin the salmon and cut into ½ inch (1 cm) cubes. Heat the olive oil in a sauté pan, add in the garlic, cook on a medium heat for a minute or so, then add the salmon and toss gently until it changes colour. Add the blanched peas. Season with salt, freshly ground pepper and sugar.

Drain the penne and toss in the 2 tablespoons of olive oil and the ½ oz of melted butter. Add the salmon mixture, the parsley and freshly squeezed lemon juice, toss gently, taste and correct the seasoning. Put into a hot serving dish, sprinkle with a little extra chopped parsley and eat immediately.

ᵛ Sugar Peas or Snow Peas

B *eware, beware! These can go on cooking after they've been drained, so err on the side of undercooking.*

1 lb (450 g) sugar peas, sugar
    snaps *or* snow peas
2 pints (1.1 L/5 cups) water
1½ teasp. salt
1–2 ozs (30–55 g/¼–½ stick)
    butter

Serves 6

String the sugar peas. Bring the water to a good rolling boil, add the salt and the peas and continue to boil furiously with the lid off until just cooked: they should still have a slight crunch. Drain immediately,* toss in the melted butter, taste and correct seasoning. Serve immediately in a hot serving dish.

*Like many green vegetables, sugar peas or snow peas can be refreshed with cold water at this point and reheated in boiling salted water just before serving (see page 99).

Peppers and Chillies

If you want to bring the strong colours and sunny flavours of the Mediterranean into your kitchen at any time, reach for a dazzling variety of peppers. Unlike so many vegetables, they are usually in good condition all year round and can be put to all sorts of interesting uses. Roasting or chargrilling intensifies the sweetness which is most pronounced in the red and yellow varieties. For many people, a roast red and yellow pepper salad has already become an addiction.

Chillies, the new must-have flavouring for switched-on cooks, often provoke fear and dread because it can be difficult to know just how hot a recipe may turn out to be. The main thing to remember is that you are in control, so you don't necessarily *have* to add as many chillies as specified. But do experiment, because chillies really can add spice to your life. Included in this book are French Beans with Chilli (page 14), Calabrese with Chilli and Garlic (page 23) and Onion Bhajis with Tomato and Chilli Sauce (page 91).

There are many different kinds – as a general rule the smaller the type of chilli, the hotter it is – but so far most of those available in Ireland are Dutch, and measure only about four on the red-hot Richter scale! If you need more information I recommend *The Great Chilli Book* by Mark Miller (Ten Speed Press, California).

v * Roast Red Pepper, Lentil and Goat's Cheese Salad

4 red peppers, roasted, peeled, deseeded and chopped (see page 104)
8 ozs (225 g/1 generous cup) Lentils du Puy
1 carrot
1 onion, stuck with 2 cloves

bouquet garni
extra virgin olive oil
a large handful of finely chopped fresh herbs – fresh annual marjoram *or* parsley
freshly squeezed lemon juice
sea salt and freshly ground pepper

sundried tomatoes in oil
(optional)
a little Irish goat's cheese –
St Tola, Cais Cleire *or*
Maughnaclea

Garnish
rocket leaves

Serves 6

W ash the lentils, put them into a large saucepan, cover with cold water, add the carrot, onion and bouquet garni, bring slowly to the boil, reduce heat and simmer very gently for 10-15 minutes, testing regularly. The lentils should be *al dente* but not hard. Drain, remove and discard the carrot, onion and bouquet garni. Season the lentils while still warm with some extra virgin olive oil, then add the finely chopped herbs and lots of freshly squeezed lemon juice. Season with sea salt and freshly ground pepper, taste and correct the seasoning.

While the lentils are still warm, arrange on a plate or plates, top with freshly roasted red pepper, some slices of perfect Irish goat's cheese, perhaps a few sundried tomatoes and garnish with rocket leaves. Serve warm.

* SUNDRIED TOMATOES

S *undried tomatoes are all the rage now in both Italy and France. They can be bought at enormous expense preserved in olive oil but you can make your own quite easily. I find this method of drying them in the coolest oven of my 4-door Aga very successful. A fan oven works well also.*

very ripe tomatoes
sea salt
sugar
olive oil

Cut the tomatoes in half cross-ways, put on to a wire rack, season with sea salt and sugar and drizzle with olive oil. Leave in the coolest part of a 4-door Aga, or in a fan oven at the minimum temperature, until they are totally dried out and wizened. I leave them in for 12-24 hours depending on size (after about 8 hours turn them upside down).

Store in sterilised jars covered with olive oil. A few basil leaves or a couple of sprigs of rosemary, thyme or annual marjoram added to the oil make them especially delicious.

Cover and keep in a cool, dry, preferably dark place. Use on salads, with pasta etc.

vv* Chargrilled Red and Yellow Peppers

T *he sweet, slightly smoky flavour of roast or chargrilled peppers makes this summery starter one of my absolute favourites. In fact every now and then I roast lots of peppers and store them peeled and deseeded in a glass Kilner jar with a*

*few fresh basil leaves and lots of extra
virgin olive oil. Then I can dip in
whenever I fancy and eat them as they
are, or use them in a salad or as an
accompaniment to pangrilled fish or meat,
or with lentils and goat's cheese as in the
previous recipe.*

**8 each fleshy red and yellow
    peppers (preferably Italian *or*
    Spanish)
2 cloves of garlic cut in very fine
    slivers (optional)
8 fresh basil leaves
extra virgin olive oil
10-12 black Kalamati olives
    (optional)
sea salt and freshly cracked
    pepper**

Serves 8

Preheat the grill or better still use a
charcoal grill. Grill the peppers on all
sides, turning them when necessary,
until they are quite charred.
Alternatively preheat the oven to
250°C/475°F/regulo 9. Put the
peppers on a baking tray and bake for
20-30 minutes until they are soft and
the skin blisters. Put them into a
plastic bag to cool and seal the end –
this will make them much easier to
peel.

    Peel the peppers and remove
stalks and seeds – don't wash. Choose
a wide, shallow serving dish. Arrange
the peeled peppers, add the garlic
slivers, fresh basil and a good drizzle
of olive oil. Scatter a few black olives
over the top if liked. Serve with
Bruschetta as a first course.

    Bruschetta: Slices of thick Italian
white country bread chargrilled or
toasted on each side, rubbed with
garlic when hot, then drizzled with
extra virgin olive oil.

Piedmontese Peppers

E lizabeth David introduced me to this
recipe in her book Italian Food, *first
published by Macdonald in 1954. Her
version is similar to the one served by
Simon Hopkinson at Bibendum in
London.*

**4 fat fleshy red peppers, Spanish
    if available
4-5 cloves of garlic
8 very ripe small tomatoes,
    peeled
16 anchovy fillets
extra virgin olive oil**

**salt, freshly ground pepper and
    sugar**

Garnish
fresh basil leaves
Serves 8

Cut the peppers in half lengthwise
through the stalk and remove the
seeds but leave the stalk attached.
Arrange the peppers skin-side down
on a low-sided baking tray. Into each
pepper put 2 or 3 slivers of garlic and
half an anchovy fillet cut into pieces.

Put a peeled tomato on top, season with salt, freshly ground pepper and a pinch of sugar. Criss-cross with 2 anchovies over the top of each tomato and drizzle with a little extra virgin olive oil. Season with salt, freshly ground pepper and a pinch of sugar.

Cook in a preheated oven, 180°C/350°F/regulo 4, for 30-45 minutes. Serve warm or cold garnished with fresh basil leaves.

ᵛ* Red Pepper Tart

A *very delicious tart, perfect for a starter or a summer lunch.*

Shortcrust Pastry
4 ozs (110 g) flour
2 ozs (55 g/½ stick) butter
water *or* beaten egg to bind
2-3 red peppers, Spanish if available
1-2 tablesp. sunflower oil
salt and freshly ground pepper
1 egg
1 egg yolk
8 fl ozs (250 ml/1 cup) cream
fresh basil leaves (optional)
quiche tin with removable base, 7½ inch (19 cm) diameter × 1¼ inches (3 cm) high

Serves 4-6

Preheat the oven to 180°C/350°F/regulo 4. Line a flan ring with the pastry, cover the pastry with kitchen or greaseproof paper and fill with baking beans and prebake in a moderate oven for 15-20 minutes. Remove the beans and paper and allow to cool.

Quarter the peppers, remove the seeds and cut the flesh into ½ inch (1 cm) dice approx. Heat the oil in a stainless steel saucepan, sweat the pepper until soft but not coloured, season with salt and freshly ground pepper. Allow to cool.

Whisk the egg and egg yolk with the cream, add the peppers and a few leaves of torn basil if you wish. Pour into the pastry case and bake in a moderate oven for 30-35 minutes or until just set and slightly golden on top. Serve with a salad of rocket leaves or a good green salad.

Potatoes

^v Potato, Onion and Lovage Soup
^v Potato and Scallion Salad
^{vv} Crispy Roast Potatoes
^v Elizabeth's Cheesy Potatoes
Salmon and Potato Cakes
Crispy Salmon and Potato Cakes
^v Tortilla de Patatas
^{v*} Rumbledethumps
^v Heaven and Earth
^v Parmesan and Olive Oil Mash

Potatoes have come a long way since they were introduced to Ireland by Sir Walter Raleigh, who is said to have planted the first potato in his garden at Myrtle Grove in Youghal in 1585. Stephen Switzer, an English garden designer and seedsman to the aristocracy, said in 1733: 'That which was heretofore reckoned a food fit only for Irishmen and clowns has now become the diet of the most luxuriously polite.'

He would be even more amused now to see the once humble spud starring on restaurant menus, since it is suddenly fashionable to specify the particular variety that is served. In Britain specialist growers haven't been able to keep up with the demand from restaurants for the older varieties, such is the swing away from the watery, nitrogen-boosted horrors to which ordinary consumers are being subjected more and more.

In the last few years I have been growing a number of old varieties myself. My favourites include Pink Fir Apple, Sharp's Express, Irene, Ratte, Charlotte and Skerry Champions. They are so delicious that we eat them on their own with butter, as a main course! These old varieties can be difficult for gardeners to find, but enthusiasts pass them on to each other. For further information contact Brian O'Donnell, Teagasc, Raphoe, Lifford, Co. Donegal, tel. 074 45490/45488.

If you don't grow your own, do at least make sure that the potatoes you buy still have the soil on, as they will taste better and keep longer than those dreadful, soap-flavoured washed potatoes in plastic bags which are creeping into supermarkets like a virus. Also, be sure to store your potatoes in a dark place, as light turns them green and toxic.

There are so many exciting ways to cook potatoes, apart from boiling or roasting them, that I could dedicate a whole book to the subject!

In my last book, *Simply Delicious Food for Family & Friends*, I included a large variety of potato recipes, but I've put some more enticing ones in here to tempt you further.

^v Potato, Onion and Lovage Soup

L ucy Madden of Hilton Park in Co. Monaghan gave me this lovely soup recipe. Lovage is a perennial herb with a distinct celery flavour.

3 potatoes, thinly sliced
½-1 oz (15-30 g/1-2 American tablesp.) butter
3 onions, very thinly sliced
salt and freshly ground pepper
2 pints (1.1 L/5 cups) good homemade chicken *or* vegetable stock
3 tablesp. approx. lovage leaves

Garnish
lovage and parsley

Serves 6

Melt the butter in a heavy-bottomed saucepan on a low heat, add the onions and potatoes, season with salt and freshly ground pepper and sweat until soft but not coloured. Add the stock and boil for 5 minutes.

Roll up a bunch of lovage leaves and cut into thin strips with scissors. Put 3 tablespoons into the soup and cook for a further 10 minutes. Taste and correct the seasoning. Serve with a sprinkling of snipped lovage and a little fresh parsley.

^v Potato and Scallion Salad

T he secret of a really delicious potato salad is to season well and to toss the potatoes in the dressing while they are still hot.

2 lbs (900 g) freshly cooked potatoes, diced (allow about 2¼ lbs/1.1 kg raw potatoes)
1 tablesp. approx. chopped parsley

2 tablesp. approx. chopped scallions *or* chives
salt and freshly ground pepper
4 fl ozs (120 ml/½ cup) French Dressing (see page 42)
4 fl ozs (120 ml/½ cup) homemade Mayonnaise (see page 30)

Serves 6

The potatoes should be boiled in their jackets and peeled, diced and measured while still hot. Mix immediately with the parsley, scallions, salt and freshly ground pepper. Stir in the French Dressing, allow to cool and finally add the homemade Mayonnaise. This keeps well for about 2 days but is best when freshly made.

ᵛᵛ Crispy Roast Potatoes

Everybody loves roast potatoes, yet people ask me over and over again for the secret of golden crispiness.

Well, first and foremost buy good quality 'old' potatoes – Golden Wonders, Kerr's Pinks, Penella or British Queens. New potatoes are not suitable for roasting.

Peel the potatoes just before roasting. Do not leave them soaking in water or they will become soggy inside because of the water they absorb. If they must be prepared ahead, put the peeled potatoes into a bowl lined with wet kitchen paper, and cover the potatoes with a thick layer of the same. Dry potatoes thoroughly before roasting, otherwise they will stick to the tin, and when they are turned over you will lose the crispy bit underneath.

If you have a fan oven it is necessary to blanch and refresh the potatoes first. Heat the olive oil or fat in a roasting tin and toss the potatoes to make sure they are well coated in olive oil. Roast in a hot oven, 230°C/450°F/regulo 8, basting occasionally, for 30–60 minutes depending on size.

For perfection, potatoes should be similar in size and shape.

ᵛᵛ ROAST POTATOES WITH ROSEMARY

Add a few sprigs of rosemary to the olive oil for roasting the potatoes, sprinkle with sea salt and garnish with fresh rosemary sprigs.

ᵛ Elizabeth's Cheesy Potatoes

A great way to use up left-over potatoes, given to me by my sister Elizabeth.

1 lb (450 g/2½ cups) cold boiled potatoes, peeled and cut into ¾ inch (2 cm) dice

¼ pint (150 ml/generous ½ cup) cold milk
salt and freshly ground pepper
4 ozs (110 g/1 cup) Irish Cheddar cheese, grated

greased pie dish, 1 pint
(600 ml/2½ cup) capacity

Serves 2-3

Put the diced potatoes into a
saucepan, add the cold milk and
season with salt and freshly ground
pepper. Stir over a low heat until the
potatoes have absorbed the milk, then
add 3 ozs (85 g) of the grated cheese,
stir gently and turn into a pie dish.
Sprinkle the remaining grated cheese
over the top. Cook in a moderate
oven, 180°C/350°F/regulo 4, until
nicely brown on top – 25 minutes
approx.

Note: Some potatoes will absorb
more milk than others. If the mixture
looks a bit dry, add a little more milk.

These potatoes are delicious
served with fish. The recipe can be
varied slightly by adding some
chopped cooked smoked ham or
rasher, or a little sautéed onion.

Salmon and Potato Cakes

F*ish cakes, which used to be relegated
to end-of-week suppers, are all the
rage again and are now popping up on
trendy restaurant menus. I'm not a bit
surprised! Left-over mashed or Duchesse
potato may be used.*

1 lb (450 g) unpeeled 'old'
potatoes – Golden Wonders
or Kerr's Pinks
10 ozs (285 g) cooked salmon
1 beaten egg, preferably
free-range
1-2 ozs (30-55 g/¼-½ stick)
butter
1 tablesp. approx. chopped
parsley
2 tablesp. approx. chopped
spring onion
2 tablesp. approx. freshly
chopped coriander
salt, freshly ground pepper and
nutmeg
creamy milk

seasoned flour
olive oil *or* butter for frying

Serves 10

Cook the salmon in boiling salted
water, allow to cool, skin and remove
the bones. Meanwhile cook the
potatoes in their jackets, pull off the
peel and mash right away. Add one
beaten egg, butter, herbs and flaked
salmon. Season with lots of salt and
freshly ground pepper and a little
nutmeg, adding a few drops of
creamy milk if the mixture is too stiff.
Taste and correct the seasoning.

Shape into cakes, approximately
3 inches (7.5 cm) in diameter and a
scant 1 inch (2.5 cm) thick. Dip in
seasoned flour.

Melt some butter or olive oil in a
frying pan on a gentle heat. Fry the
salmon and potato cakes until golden
on one side, then flip over and cook

on the other side, 4–5 minutes approx. each side; they should be crusty and golden.

Serve on hot plates with a blob of Garlic Butter (see page 91) melting on top.

Crispy Salmon and Potato Cakes

Flour, egg and crumb the salmon and potato cakes, and deep or shallow fry until crispy. Serve with Tartare Sauce and a segment of lemon.

ᵛ Tortilla de Patatas (Spanish Potato Omelette)

In Spain, you must understand, Tortilla is not just a dish – it is a way of life. Tortillas are loved by Spaniards and tourists alike. You'll be offered them in every home, in the most elegant restaurants and the most run down establishments. No picnic would be complete without a tortilla, every tapas bar will have appetising wedges on display, and people even eat it at the cinema!

Tortilla de Patatas sounds deceptively simple, but it's not as easy to make to perfection as you might think.

8 ozs (225 g) potatoes, thinly sliced
5 ozs (140 g/generous 1 cup) onions, thinly sliced
8 eggs, preferably free-range
1 teasp. approx. sea salt
Spanish olive oil, e.g. Lerida

frying pan, 7-8 inch (18-20.5 cm) diameter (nonstick if possible)

Serves 6

Put a generous 1 inch (2.5 cm) of olive oil into a frying pan and cook the onions and sliced potatoes over a medium heat until crisp and golden. This can take up to 20 minutes. Drain off the oil and reserve to use another time.

Whisk the eggs in a bowl, season with the salt, add the potato and onion. Put 2 tablespoons of oil back into the pan. When it begins to sizzle pour in the egg mixture, then lower the heat. Loosen around the edge when the eggs begin to set, and continue to cook, shaking the pan occasionally.

When the tortilla is well set and golden underneath, cover the pan with a plate and turn it out, taking care not to burn your hand. Add a little more oil to the frying pan if necessary. Slide the tortilla back in, cooked side uppermost. Cook until firm but still slightly moist in the centre. Serve hot or at room temperature, cut into wedges.

ᵛ* Rumbledethumps

All cultures that have cabbage and potatoes put them together in some form. In Ireland we have Colcannon, in England Bubble and Squeak, but the Scottish version is called Rumbledethumps.

1 lb (450 g) potatoes, freshly mashed
8 ozs (225 g) kale *or* spring cabbage, thinly shredded
¼ pint (150 ml/generous ½ cup) cream
1 tablesp. approx. chopped spring onion

salt and freshly ground black pepper
butter (optional)

Serves 4

Cook the cabbage or kale in a little boiling salted water and drain well.

Put the cream into a large pot with the spring onion, bring slowly to the boil, and add the potatoes and freshly cooked cabbage. Season with salt and freshly ground pepper. Beat the mixture with a wooden spoon for 1-2 minutes and taste. You could add a lump of butter if you like – the Scots do!

ᵛ Heaven and Earth

In this German recipe the apples represent heaven and the potatoes earth. It's particularly good served with pork, bacon and black pudding.

2 lbs (900 g) floury potatoes
1 lb (450 g) cooking apples
1 tablesp. approx. sugar
salt and freshly ground pepper
1-2 ozs (30-55 g/¼-½ stick) butter

Serves 4

Boil the potatoes in their jackets. Meanwhile peel and cook the apples in a little water with the sugar until soft and fluffy. When the potatoes are cooked pull off the skins quickly and mash them together with the apples. Season with salt, freshly ground pepper and a good lump of butter. Taste and add more sugar if necessary. Serve piping hot.

^vParmesan and Olive Oil Mash

F*resh chicken livers cooked in a little butter with some fresh sage leaves are delicious served on top of the following recipe.*

2 lbs (900 g) old potatoes, e.g. Golden Wonders
3 ozs (85 g/¾ stick) butter *or* extra virgin olive oil
8 fl ozs (250 ml/1 cup) approx. boiling milk
2 ozs (55 g/½ cup) freshly grated Parmesan (Parmigiano Reggiano is best)
salt and freshly ground pepper

Scrub the potatoes but do not peel them, cook in boiling salted water until they are about three-quarters cooked. Pour off most of the water, cover and steam for the rest of the cooking. Meanwhile bring the milk to the boil and add the butter or olive oil. Peel the potatoes as soon as they are cooked and mash or purée through a 'potato ricer'. Beat in half of the hot milk, add the Parmesan cheese and finally the remainder of the milk. The amount will depend on the variety of potato – some absorb more than others. It should be light and fluffy. Taste, correct the seasoning and serve immediately.

VARIATION
Omit the Parmesan cheese, but drizzle the top with extra virgin olive oil and garnish with a few chopped olives for extra pzazz!

Spinach and Swiss Chard

v* Buttered Spinach
v Creamed Spinach
v Oeufs Florentine
Garden Spinach Soup
Spinach and Rosemary Soup
* Pork, Spinach and Herb Terrine
v Spinach and Mushroom Pancakes
v* Swiss Chard with Parmesan

One glance at those wilting, yellowing spinach leaves in plastic bags in the greengrocers should be enough to encourage you to grow your own spinach. Nothing could be easier, and few vegetables will give you so much return for so little effort. There are two kinds: tender and delicate summer spinach, and the slightly more robust perpetual spinach which keeps going all year round. In fact, the more you eat the more it comes.

I tend to feel that, whereas summer spinach is best cooked in just the water that adheres to the leaves after washing, the more strongly flavoured perpetual variety benefits from being cooked in plenty of well salted, fast boiling water. You might also consider growing its first cousin, Swiss chard. Here you have two vegetables in one. The leaves can be cooked like spinach and the stalk like celery, served buttered or in a creamy sauce. Ruby chard, or rhubarb chard as it is sometimes called with its brilliant red stalks, has given me great joy in the winter for the past few years. It is cooked in exactly the same way as Swiss chard but it looks so beautiful in the garden that I can hardly bear to pick it.

v* Buttered Spinach

Here are three different basic methods of cooking spinach – all of them a huge improvement on the watery mush that frozen spinach often unfortunately ends up as!

2 lbs (900 g) fresh spinach, with stalks removed
salt, freshly ground pepper and a little freshly grated nutmeg
2-4 ozs (55-110 g/½-1 stick) butter

Serves 4-6

Preparation
1. Melt a scrap of the butter in a wide frying pan, toss in as much spinach as will fit easily, season with salt and freshly ground pepper. As soon as the spinach wilts and becomes tender, strain off the excess liquid, increase the heat and add some butter and freshly grated nutmeg. Serve immediately.

2. Wash the spinach and drain. Put into a heavy saucepan on a very low heat, season and cover tightly. After a few minutes, stir and replace the lid. As soon as the spinach is cooked, 5-8 minutes approx., strain off the copious amount of liquid that spinach releases and press until almost dry. Chop or purée in a food processor if you like a smooth texture. Increase the heat, add butter, correct the seasoning and add a little freshly grated nutmeg to taste.

3. Cook the spinach uncovered in a large saucepan of boiling salted water until soft, 4-5 minutes approx. Drain and press out all the water. Continue as in method 2. Method 3 produces a a more brightly coloured spinach.

^v Creamed Spinach

Cook spinach in any of the above ways and drain very well. Add 8-12 fl ozs (250-350 ml/1-1½ cups) cream to the spinach and bring to the boil, stir well and thicken with a little roux if desired, otherwise stir over the heat until the spinach has absorbed most of the cream. Season with salt, pepper and freshly grated nutmeg to taste. Creamed Spinach may be cooked ahead of time and reheated.

^v Oeufs Florentine

A classic and one of the most delicious combinations. Serve freshly poached free-range eggs on top of Creamed Spinach – one of our favourite lunch or supper dishes.

Garden Spinach Soup

The trick with these green soups is not to add the greens until the last minute, otherwise it will overcook and you will lose the fresh taste and lovely bright colour.

8-12 ozs (225-340 g/5-6 cups) spinach, chopped
2 ozs (55 g/½ stick) butter
4 ozs (110 g/1 cup) onions, chopped
5 ozs (140 g/1 cup) potatoes, chopped
salt and freshly ground pepper
1 pint (600 ml/2½ cups) homemade chicken stock
¾-1 pint (450-600 ml/2½ cups) creamy milk (¼ cream and ¾ milk)
freshly grated nutmeg

Garnish
whipped cream (optional)
freshly chopped parsley

Serves 6-8

Melt the butter in a heavy-bottomed saucepan. When it foams, add the potatoes and onions and turn them until well coated. Sprinkle with salt and freshly ground pepper. Cover and sweat on a gentle heat for 10 minutes.

Add the boiling stock and milk, bring back to the boil and cook until the potatoes and onions are soft. Add the spinach and boil *with the lid off* for 3-5 minutes approx., until the spinach is cooked. Do not overcook or the soup will lose its fresh green colour.

Liquidise, taste and add some freshly grated nutmeg. Serve in warm bowls garnished with a blob of whipped cream and some chopped parsley.

Spinach and Rosemary Soup

*A*dd 1 tablespoon of chopped fresh rosemary to the soup just before it is liquidised. Garnish with a blob of whipped cream and some rosemary.

* Pork, Spinach and Herb Terrine

This terrine tastes different every time we make it, depending on the variety of herbs used. It should be highly seasoned *before it is cooked, otherwise it may taste bland when cold.*

1½ lbs (675 g) spinach (include
    some sorrel if possible)
2 lbs (900 g) streaky pork
8 ozs (225 g) pig's liver
6 ozs (170 g) gammon *or* smoked
    lean bacon
6 ozs (170 g) streaky bacon
2 medium onions, finely chopped
½ oz (15 g/⅛ stick) butter
2 medium cloves of garlic,
    chopped
2 beaten eggs, preferably
    free-range
salt, freshly ground black pepper
    and grated nutmeg to taste
4 tablesp. approx. freshly
    chopped herbs – rosemary,
    thyme, basil, marjoram,
    parsley, chives
2 terrines *or* 2 8 × 4 inch (20.5 ×
    10 cm) loaf tins

Makes 2 loaves of pâté
Serves 20 approx.

Mince the meat. Sweat the finely
chopped onions in the butter. String
and cook the spinach as for Buttered
Spinach (see page 113) until soft,
drain well and chop it up. Mix all the
ingredients together thoroughly,
adding seasoning and herbs to taste.
Fry a little piece of the mixture on a
pan, taste and correct the seasoning if
necessary.

    Put into two terrines, cover with
a lid or tin foil and bake for 1 hour
approx. in a preheated oven, 180°C/
350°F/regulo 4. Remove the cover
approx. 15 minutes before the end of
cooking time, to allow the top to
brown.

    Serve warm or cold.

ᵛ Spinach and Mushroom Pancakes

*There are lots of variations on this
theme, but this is a particularly
delicious version.*

1 lb (450 g) spinach
1 × **Mushroom à la Crème recipe**
    (see page 87)

Pancake Batter
5 ozs (140 g/1 cup) flour
good pinch of salt
3 eggs, preferably free-range
8 fl ozs (250 ml/1 cup) milk
4 fl ozs (120 ml/generous ½ cup)
    water

2-3 tablesp. approx. olive oil *or*
    melted butter

Serves 6-8

To make the pancakes: Sieve the flour
and salt into a bowl, whisk the eggs
lightly, make a well in the centre of
the flour, add in the eggs, milk and
water, and draw in the flour gradually
from the sides using a whisk. Add the
oil or melted butter and leave the
batter to rest for 30 minutes-1 hour.
Cook small ladlefuls of the batter on a
hot non-stick pan and keep aside.

Remove the stalks from the spinach and cook as for Buttered Spinach (see page 113). Mix the Mushroom à la Crème with the spinach. Taste and correct the seasoning.

Lay a pancake on a clean worktop. Put about 2 tablespoons of filling in the middle, fold in two sides and fold over the ends into a parcel. Repeat with the others. If the components are cold, reheat in a covered dish in a moderate oven. Serve with a little light Hollandaise Sauce (see page 2).

^{v*} Swiss Chard with Parmesan

There are several ways of using chard stalks, including tossing them in vinaigrette or olive oil and lemon juice or serving them in a Mornay Sauce. This way is particularly delicious, however, and it also works well with Florence fennel and courgettes which have first been blanched, refreshed and sliced. Intersperse the courgettes with a few leaves of basil if available.

1 lb (450 g) Swiss chard stalks
salt and freshly ground pepper
butter
3 ozs (85 g) freshly grated
  Parmesan cheese, preferably
  Parmigiano Reggiano

lasagne dish, 8 × 10 inch
  (20.5 × 25 cm)

Serves 4

Cut the chard stalks into pieces 4 inches (10 cm) long approx. Save the green leaves to cook at another time as you would spinach. Cook the stalks in boiling salted water until they feel tender when pierced with the tip of a knife. Drain.

Smear the dish with a little butter; arrange some of the chard stalks in a single layer, season with salt and freshly ground pepper, sprinkle some Parmesan cheese and dot with a little butter. Repeat until the dish is full. Finally sprinkle the top layer generously with Parmesan cheese and dot with butter.

Bake in a preheated oven, 200°C/400°F/regulo 6, for 15-20 minutes or until crisp and golden.

117

Sweetcorn

*v** *Sweetcorn with Butter and Sea Salt*

The only way you are likely to taste sweetcorn at its most exquisite is if you grow your own, or have a close and kind neighbour who does – because sweetcorn should be cooked within minutes of being picked. That's why, at roadside stalls selling corn in the United States, there is a big clock indicating the time at which it was harvested!

*v** Sweetcorn with Butter and Sea Salt

4 ears of sweetcorn, for
    perfection just picked
3-4 ozs (85–110 g/¾–1 stick)
    butter
sea salt

Serves 4

Bring a large saucepan of water to a fast rolling boil and add lots of salt. Peel the husks and silks off the sweetcorn, trim the ends, put into the boiling water, bring back to the boil and cook for 3 minutes. Serve immediately with butter and sea salt.

Tomatoes

v *Tomato and Mint Soup*
vv* *Red and Yellow Tomato Salad with Mint or Basil*
v* *Tomato and Basil Tart*
v *Tomato and Pesto Omelette*
Penne all'Arrabbiata
Salmon with Tomato, Ginger and Fresh Coriander
Chicken Breast with Tomato and Basil Sauce

I used to think the flavour of the Irish tomatoes that appear in the shops towards the end of the summer was incomparable, but now I'm not so sure. Various long-life varieties which remain rock hard and fairly flavourless for weeks are beginning to appear on the shelves. With shelf life in mind, commercial growers are obliged to pick their tomatoes while they are still underripe – and tomatoes that have ripened in a box just don't taste the same as those which have reached maturity on the vine.

All of this means that it's more worthwhile than ever to grow a few tomatoes yourself. For guaranteed success, given the unreliability of Irish summer weather, you will probably need a greenhouse. If you have one, buy a couple of grow bags and a few plants, and for part of the year at least you will be able to enjoy some tomatoes that taste the way tomatoes should.

If you don't have a greenhouse, you might still like to try growing some of the small varieties like Tumbler and Sweet 100s in hanging baskets at the kitchen door, as I did last year. They are ideal for anybody who wants to do a little gentle gardening without much spadework.

If you have to rely on what is in the shops, remember that colour is a good indicator of flavour, so choose dark red tomatoes if possible. If the tomatoes you buy aren't dark red, keep them in the kitchen for a few days (*not* in the fridge!) and the flavour will develop. Do buy Irish, because our tomatoes have more flavour than many of the imported ones and are grown in fairly natural conditions, without much use of fertiliser or chemicals. At the end of the summer they are so cheap that it's worth buying a box, and making chutney and Tomato Purée by the gallon – a marvellous freezer standby.

^v Tomato and Mint Soup

We worked for a long time to try and make this soup reasonably foolproof. Good quality tinned tomatoes (a must for your store cupboard) give a really good result but because they are rather more acidic than fresh you need to add sugar. Homemade Tomato Purée, although delicious, can give a more variable result depending on the quality of the tomatoes.

1¼ pints (750 ml/3 cups) homemade Tomato Purée (see page 90) or 2 × 14 oz (400 g) tins of tomatoes, liquidised and sieved + 2 teasp. sugar
1 onion, finely chopped
½ oz (15 g/⅛ stick) butter
8 fl ozs (250 ml/1 cup) Béchamel Sauce (see below)
8 fl ozs (250 ml/1 cup) homemade chicken stock or vegetable stock
2 tablesp. approx. freshly chopped mint
salt and freshly ground pepper
1-2 tablesp. (1½-2½ American tablesp.) sugar if using tinned tomatoes
4 fl ozs (120 ml/½ cup) cream

Garnish
whipped cream
fresh mint leaves

Serves 5

Sweat the onion in the butter on a gentle heat until soft but not coloured. Add the Tomato Purée or chopped tinned tomatoes plus juice, the Béchamel Sauce and homemade chicken or vegetable stock. Add the chopped mint, season with salt, pepper and all the sugar if you are using tinned tomatoes – otherwise just a pinch. Bring to the boil and simmer for a few minutes.

Liquidise, taste and dilute further if necessary. Bring back to the boil, correct the seasoning and serve with the addition of a little cream. Garnish with a tiny blob of whipped cream and some mint.

Note: This soup needs to be tasted carefully as the final result depends on the quality of the Tomato Purée, stock etc.

BÉCHAMEL SAUCE
½ pint (300 ml/1¼ cups) milk
a few slices of carrot
a few slices of onion
3 peppercorns
small sprig of thyme
small sprig of parsley
1½ ozs (45 g/scant ⅓ cup) roux (see glossary)
salt and freshly ground pepper

This is a wonderfully quick way of making Béchamel Sauce if you have roux already made. Put the cold milk into a saucepan with the carrot, onion, peppercorns, thyme and parsley. Bring to the boil, simmer for

4–5 minutes, remove from the heat and leave to infuse for 10 minutes. Strain out the vegetables, bring the milk back to the boil and thicken to a

light coating consistency by whisking in the roux. Add salt and freshly ground pepper, taste and correct the seasoning if necessary.

vv* Red and Yellow Tomato Salad with Mint or Basil

In the late summer when we have intensely sweet vine ripened tomatoes we often serve a tomato salad as a first course. The flavour is so wonderful it is a revelation to many people who have forgotten what a tomato should taste like.

For 6 very ripe firm red or a mixture of red and yellow tomatoes
1–2 teasp. chopped fresh mint *or* torn basil
salt, freshly ground black pepper and sugar
French Dressing (see below)

Serves 4

Remove the core from each tomato and slice into 3 or 4 rounds (around the equator) or into quarters. Arrange in a single layer on a flat plate. Sprinkle with salt, sugar and several grinds of black pepper. Toss immediately in just enough French Dressing to coat the tomatoes, and sprinkle with chopped mint or torn basil. Taste for seasoning. Tomatoes must be dressed as soon as they are cut to seal in their flavour.

FRENCH DRESSING
2 fl ozs (60 ml/¼ cup) wine vinegar
6 fl ozs (175 ml/¾ cup) extra virgin olive oil *or* a mixture of olive and other oils, e.g. sunflower and arachide
1 level teasp. (½ American teasp.) mustard (Dijon *or* English)
1 large clove of garlic
1 scallion *or* spring onion
sprig of parsley
sprig of watercress
1 level teasp. (½ American teasp.) salt
a few grinds of pepper

Put all the ingredients into a blender and run at medium speed for 1 minute approx. Alternatively mix oil and vinegar in a bowl, add mustard, salt, freshly ground pepper and mashed garlic; chop finely the parsley, spring onion and watercress and add in. Whisk before serving.

^v* Tomato and Basil Tart

Rich Shortcrust Pastry
6 ozs (170 g) flour
3 ozs (85 g) butter
1 egg yolk
2 tablesp. approx. water

Filling
10 ozs (285 g) very ripe tomatoes
2 eggs, free range if possible
3 oz (85 g/¾ cup) grated
   Emmental *or* Gruyère cheese
3 fl oz (75 ml/scant ½ cup) cream
1 oz (30 g/¼ cup) freshly grated
   Parmesan cheese, preferably
   Parmigiano Reggiano
salt, freshly ground pepper and
   sugar
4-5 large basil leaves
1 tablesp. finely snipped chives

1 tart tin or flan ring, 8 inch
   (20.5 cm) diameter × 1¼
   (3 cm) inches deep

Serves 6

First make the pastry. Sieve the flour into a bowl and rub in the butter until the mixture resembles coarse breadcrumbs. Mix the water with the yolk, and use it to bind the pastry. Add a little more water if necessary, but don't make it too sticky. Chill for 15 minutes, then roll out to line the tart tin or flan ring to a thickness of ⅛ inch (3 mm) approx. Line with greaseproof paper and fill to the top with dried beans. Rest for 15 minutes and bake at 180°C/350°F/regulo 4 for 20 minutes. Remove beans and paper.

Next make the filling. Whisk the eggs with the cream in a bowl, add the cheese, season with salt and freshly ground black pepper to taste. Scald and peel the tomatoes and cut into ¼ inch (5 mm) rings, season with salt, freshly ground pepper and sugar. Put a few tablespoons of the custard into the pastry case and then a layer of tomato rings. Sprinkle on a layer of torn basil leaves and chopped chives. Put in the rest of the custard and top with the remaining seasoned tomato rings.

Bake at 180°C/350°F/regulo 4 for 30 minutes approx., or until the tart is just set and golden on top. Serve with a good green salad.

^v Tomato and Pesto Omelette

An omelette is the ultimate instant food but many a travesty is served in its name. The whole secret is to have the pan hot enough and to use clarified butter if at all possible. Ordinary butter will burn if your pan is as hot as it ought to be. The omelette should be made in half the time it takes to read this recipe. Your first may not be a joy to behold but persevere — practice makes perfect! Tomato and Pesto filling makes a sublime omelette.

2 eggs, preferably free-range
1 dessertsp. (2 American teasp.)
  water *or* milk
salt and freshly ground pepper
1 dessertsp. (2 American teasp.)
  clarified butter (see glossary)
  ***or* olive oil**
1 tablesp. approx. Pesto
  (see page 7)
2 tablesp. approx. Tomato
  Fondue (see page 15)

omelette pan, 9 inch (23 cm)
  diameter, preferably non-stick

Serves 1

Warm a plate in the oven. Whisk the eggs with the water or milk in a bowl with a fork, or whisk until thoroughly mixed but not too fluffy. Season with the salt and freshly ground pepper. Put the warm plate beside the cooker. Heat the omelette pan over a high heat and add the clarified butter or oil. As soon as it sizzles, pour the egg mixture into the pan. It will start to cook immediately, so quickly pull the edges of the omelette towards the centre with a metal spoon or spatula, tilting the pan so that the uncooked egg runs to the sides. Continue until most of the egg is set and will not run any more, then leave the omelette to cook for a further 10 seconds to brown the bottom.

Spoon the hot Tomato Fondue along the centre of the omelette and spread a little Pesto over it.

To fold the omelette: Flip the edge just below the handle of the pan into the centre, then hold the pan almost perpendicular over the plate so that the omelette will flip over again, then half roll, half slide the omelette on to the plate so that it lands folded into three.

The entire cooking process shouldn't take more than 30 seconds in all – perhaps 45 if you are adding a filling!

Penne all'Arrabbiata

*A*rrabbiata – literally 'angry' – pasta which means it's hot and spicy. I ate this version at the house of an Italian friend, Jo Bettoja, in Rome. Increase or decrease the amount of chilli pepper flakes depending on how 'angry' you like it. This is an excellent party pasta and will serve 20 people as part of a buffet.

2¼ lbs (1.1 kg) penne *or* similar
  tube pasta
3 tablesp. (4 American tablesp.)
  olive oil
8 ozs (225 g/1½ cups) onions,
  chopped
4 cloves of garlic, crushed
8 ozs (225 g) pancetta *or* streaky
  bacon, cut in thin julienne
  strips

4½ × 14 oz (400 g) cans chopped
   Italian plum tomatoes
salt, pepper, sugar and hot red
   chilli pepper flakes, to taste
8 ozs (225 g) grated Pecorino *or*
   Parmesan cheese, preferably
   Parmigiano Reggiano

Serves 12 as a starter

Bring the water for the pasta to a fast
rolling boil. Choose a saucepan large
enough to hold both the sauce and
pasta when it is cooked. In it heat the
oil, add the onions and garlic and
cook until lightly browned. Add the
pancetta or streaky bacon and sauté
until lightly browned but not crisp.
Add the chopped tomatoes, season
with salt, pepper, sugar and a
generous amount of pepper flakes –
the sauce should be *piccante*. Cook
uncovered until the sauce reduces
and thickens, 20 minutes approx.

   To serve, cook the penne in
boiling salted water until *al dente*,
10-12 minutes approx. Drain and add
to the hot tomato sauce. Mix on a
low heat and add the grated Pecorino
or Parmesan cheese. Serve at once.

Salmon with Tomato, Ginger and Fresh Coriander

*C laudia Roden first introduced me to
this recipe. It sounds like an
extraordinary combination but do try it.
It's delicious hot or cold.*

1½ lbs (675 g) fresh wild salmon
   fillet
a tiny dash of olive oil
2-4 cloves of garlic, peeled and
   finely chopped
8 very ripe Irish tomatoes, peeled
   and chopped
1 tablesp. approx. freshly grated
   ginger
salt, freshly ground pepper and
   sugar
2 tablesp. fresh coriander leaves

Garnish
fresh coriander leaves

Serves 6

Cut the salmon into 6 even-sized
pieces. Put the dash of olive oil in a
wide stainless steel sauté pan, add the
chopped garlic and chopped tomatoes
and cook over a medium heat until
the tomatoes soften and break down,
10-15 minutes approx. Add the
grated ginger and cook for a further
5 minutes or more. Season with salt,
pepper and a little sugar. Turn off the
heat and allow the sauce to sit until
you need it.

   Cook the salmon gently in a little
butter in a wide frying pan.*

   Just before serving, reheat the
sauce, add the coriander, cook for a
minute or two and spoon the sauce
over the salmon on hot plates.
Garnish with fresh coriander leaves
and serve immediately.

   *Alternatively, put the salmon
into the sauce, cover and cook gently
in the sauce.

Chicken Breast with Tomato and Basil Sauce

*T*his recipe has a very rich but irresistible sauce which is also delicious served with pork fillet, poached trout or monkfish.

6 chicken breasts
1 oz (30 g/¼ stick) butter
salt and freshly ground pepper

Tomato and Basil Sauce
8 fl ozs (250 ml/1 cup) cream
6 ozs (175 g/1½ sticks) butter
4 firm ripe Irish tomatoes
salt, freshly ground pepper and
**   sugar**
10–15 basil leaves, chopped

Garnish
sprigs of fresh basil, flat parsley *or*
**   chervil**

Serves 6

First make the sauce. Put the cream into a heavy saucepan over a gentle heat until it thickens and is in danger of burning. Whisk in the butter in small cubes until it is all incorporated; it should be a light coating consistency (add warm water to thin if necessary). Peel the tomatoes, quarter them and remove the seeds.

Cut the tomato flesh into ½ inch (1 cm) dice and season with salt, pepper and sugar. Add this to the sauce with the chopped basil leaves. Keep this sauce in a warm place and reheat very gently if necessary.

Heat a cast iron grill pan until quite hot. Smear the chicken breasts with a little butter and season with salt and freshly ground pepper. Place the breasts on the hot grill pan and allow to become golden brown. Turn the breasts and lightly brown the other side.

Transfer to a moderately hot oven, 180°C/350°F/regulo 4, for 10 minutes. To test if the chicken is cooked, pierce the flesh at the thickest part; if there is no trace of pink and the juices run clear, the chicken is ready. Be careful not to overcook – it should be moist and juicy. Remove from the oven and keep warm.

To serve, spoon some of the warm Tomato and Basil Sauce on to individual plates. Thinly slice each chicken breast, and while retaining the shape of the breast, carefully transfer the slices to each plate and fan them out slightly.

Turnips

Swede Turnip and Bacon Soup
ᵛ Swede Turnips with Caramelised Onions
ᵛ Braised White Turnips with Annual Marjoram

Probably because it was introduced to Ireland as cattle feed, the swede turnip has humble connotations which it is still struggling to overcome. It is beginning to get a boost, however – for the unpretentious turnip is one of the vegetables which are now all the rage as the trend towards gutsy rustic food gathers momentum.

Besides being incredibly good value, turnip is much more versatile than many people suspect. If you are going to serve it mashed in the usual way, perk it up with caramelised onions, but also try Swede Turnip and Bacon Soup which brings all of our best traditions together. Remember that farmers always say swede turnips taste best after they have had a touch of frost.

The white turnip and its first cousin, kohlrabi, are also dreadfully undervalued, so grow them if you can and don't just relegate them to the stock pot. At least try Braised White Turnips with Annual Marjoram.

Swede Turnip and Bacon Soup

12 ozs (340 g/3 cups) swede
    turnips, diced
1 tablesp. approx. sunflower *or*
    arachide oil
5 ozs (140 g) rindless streaky
    bacon cut in ½ inch (1 cm)
    dice
4 ozs (110 g/1 cup) onions,
    chopped
5 ozs (140 g/1 cup) potatoes,
    diced
salt and freshly ground pepper
1½ pints (900 ml) homemade
    chicken stock
cream *or* creamy milk to taste

Garnish
fried diced bacon
tiny croûtons
chopped parsley

Serves 6-8

Heat the oil in a saucepan, add the bacon and cook on a gentle heat until crisp and golden. Remove to a plate with a slotted spoon. Toss the onion, potato and turnip in the bacon fat, season with salt and freshly ground pepper. Cover with a butter wrapper to keep in the steam, and sweat on a gentle heat until soft but not coloured, 10 minutes approx. Add the stock, bring to the boil and simmer until the vegetables are fully cooked. Liquidise, taste, add a little cream or creamy milk and some extra seasoning if necessary.

Serve with a mixture of crispy bacon, tiny croûtons and chopped parsley sprinkled on top.

ᵛ Swede Turnips with Caramelised Onions

2 lbs (900 g) swede turnips
salt and lots of freshly ground
    pepper
2-4 ozs (55-110 g/½-1 stick)
    butter

Garnish
finely chopped parsley

Serves 6 approx.

Peel the turnip thickly in order to remove the outside skin completely. Cut into ¾ inch (2 cm) cubes approx. Cover with water. Add a good pinch of salt, bring to the boil and cook until soft. Strain off the excess water, mash the turnips well and beat in the butter. Taste and season with lots of freshly ground pepper and more salt if necessary. Garnish with parsley and serve piping hot.

CARAMELISED ONIONS
4 onions, thinly sliced
2-3 tablesp. (2-4 American
    tablesp.) olive oil

Heat the olive oil in a heavy saucepan. Toss in the onions and cook over a low heat for whatever length of time it takes for them to soften and caramelise to a golden brown – 30-45 minutes approx.

ᵛ Braised White Turnips with Annual Marjoram

This recipe is sensational on its own but particularly delicious with duck.

1 lb (450 g) small white turnips
a little butter
1-2 tablesp. (1½-2½ American
    tablesp.) oregano *or* annual
    marjoram
salt and freshly ground pepper

Wash and peel the white turnips. Cut into ¼ inch (5 mm) slices and cook in a little boiling salted water in a covered casserole until tender. Drain. Toss with a little butter and some chopped marjoram. Correct the seasoning and serve.

Notes